REMAINING CHALLENGES OF
THE SECOND VATICAN COUNCIL
FOR THE 21ST CENTURY

REMAINING CHALLENGES OF THE SECOND VATICAN COUNCIL FOR THE 21ST CENTURY

THE FINAL DECLARATION OF THE INTERNATIONAL CONGRESS, "DISCLOSING THE COUNCIL"

EDITED BY
CHRISTOPH BÖTTIGHEIMER
AND RENÉ DAUSNER

A Herder & Herder Book
The Crossroad Publishing Company
New York

A Herder & Herder Book
The Crossroad Publishing Company
www.crossroadpublishing.com

© 2018 by Christoph Böttigheimer and René Dausner.

Crossroad, Herder & Herder, and the crossed C logo/colophon are registered trademarks of The Crossroad Publishing Company.

All rights reserved. No part of this book may be copied, scanned, reproduced in any way, or stored in a retrieval system, or transmitted, in any form or by any means, electronic, mechanical, photocopying, recording, or otherwise, without the written permission of The Crossroad Publishing Company. For permission please write to rights@crossroadpublishing.com.

In continuation of our 200-year tradition of independent publishing, The Crossroad Publishing Company proudly offers a variety of books with strong, original voices and diverse perspectives. The viewpoints expressed in our books are not necessarily those of The Crossroad Publishing Company, any of its imprints or of its employees, executives, or owners. Although the author and publisher have made every effort to ensure that the information in this book was correct at press time, the author and publisher do not assume and hereby disclaim any liability to any party for any loss, damage, or disruption caused by errors or omissions, whether such errors or omissions result from negligence, accident, or any other cause. No claims are made or responsibility assumed for any health or other benefits.

The text of this book is set in 12/15 Adobe Garamond Pro.

Composition by Rachel Reiss
Cover design by Sophie Appel

Library of Congress Cataloging-in-Publication Data

Names: Konzil "eroffnen" (Conference) (2015 : Munich, Germany), author. | Bottigheimer, Christoph, editor. | Dausner, Rene, 1975- editor.
Title: The remaining challenges of the Second Vatican Council for the 21st century : the final declaration of the International Congress Disclosing the Council / edited by Christoph Bottigheimer and Rene Dausner.
Other titles: Vaticanum 21. English
Description: New York : Crossroad Publishing Company, 2018. | "A Herder & Herder book." | Includes bibliographical references and index.
Identifiers: LCCN 2018036869 (print) | LCCN 2018039507 (ebook) | ISBN 9780824599256 (Epub) | ISBN 9780824599263 (Mobipocket) | ISBN 9780824599232 (cloth : alk. paper) | ISBN 9780824599249 (trade paper : alk. paper)
Subjects: LCSH: Vatican Council (2nd : 1962-1965 : Basilica di San Pietro in Vaticano)--Congresses. | Catholic Church--History--21st century--Congresses. | Catholic Church--Forecasting--Congresses.
Classification: LCC BX830 1962 (ebook) | LCC BX830 1962 .K58813 2015 (print) | DDC 262/.52--dc23
LC record available at https://lccn.loc.gov/2018036869

Books published by The Crossroad Publishing Company may be purchased at special quantity discount rates for classes and institutional use. For information, please e-mail sales@CrossroadPublishing.com.

ACKNOWLEDGMENTS

The authors wish to give special thanks to the Pädagogische Stiftung Cassianeum, Donauwörth for their financial support of this project and for their endorsement of the text.

Dedicated to Cardinal Karl Lehmann (1936-2018),
Honorary President of the Congress

CONTENTS

Foreword — xi

INTRODUCTION — 1

Opening Plenary Session on the International Position of the Council's Reception — 4

Twelve Workshops — 9

Public Panel Discussion: "The Council—A New Beginning" (Karl Rahner) — 9

The "Finale" of the Congress — 11

FINAL DECLARATION OF THE INTERNATIONAL CONGRESS: "'DISCLOSING' THE COUNCIL" — 15

1. Freedom and Faith — 15
2. Theology as a Science — 16
3. Theology and the Episcopal Teaching Office — 16
4. Reform of Ecclesial Structures — 17
5. Inner-Christian Ecumenism — 18
6. The Church and Judaism — 18
7. The Claim of Revelation and the Plurality of Religions — 19
8. Interreligious Dialogue and Mission — 19
9. Liturgy and Inculturation — 20
10. Faith and Formation/Education — 20

11. The Church and the Media ... 21
12. Creation and Ecology ... 21

DOCUMENTATION OF THE TWELVE WORKSHOPS ... 25

1. Freedom and Faith ... 25
   Commentary by Marianne Heimbach-Steins, Saskia Wendel

2. Theology as Science ... 27
   Commentary by Gerhard Kruip/Alexander Loichinger

3. Theology and the Episcopal Teaching Office ... 31
   Commentary by Christoph Böttigheimer, René Dausner

4. Reform of Ecclesial Structures ... 34
   Commentary by Franz Xaver Bischof, Gerd Häfner, Johanna Rahner

5. Inner-Christian Ecumenism ... 38
   Commentary by Thomas Bremer, Maria Wernsmann

6. The Church and Judaism ... 41
   Commentary by Josef Wohlmuth, René Dausner

7. The Claim of Revelation and the Plurality of Religions ... 45
   Commentary by Klaus Müller

8. Interreligious Dialogue and Mission ... 48
   Commentary by Margit Eckholt

9. Liturgy and Inculturation ... 51
   Commentary by Benedikt Kranemann, Reinhard Hoeps

10. Faith and Formation/Education ... 54
    Commentary by Harald Schwillus

11. The Church and the Media ... 58
    Commentary by Matthias Sellmann, Bernd Trocholepczy

12. Creation and Ecology ... 61
    Commentary by Andraes Lienkamp/Georg Steins

Contents ix

    Conclusion 67
    List of Primary Signatories 69
    List of Co-Signatories 71
    Alphabetical List of Authors 75

FOREWORD

"Disclosing the Council" has been the programmatic title of the International Congress held in Munich fifty years after the end of Vatican II. More than two hundred theologians have come together to discuss the outcome of the Council and its implications for Catholic theology and the Roman Catholic Church in the twenty-first century. One visible result of the congress is the final declaration that was published originally in German; subsequently, the text also was published in a French and a Spanish translation. We are delighted to be able to present the final declaration also in English. It is, therefore, a great honor to thank the publisher Crossroad / Herder & Herder, especially Mr. Chris Myers, for their excellent cooperation. Last but not least we express our appreciation and thanks to the foundation *Pädagogische Stiftung Cassianeum* for the financial subsidy that made this publication possible.

Eichstätt (Bavaria), 15 February 2017
Christoph Böttigheimer
René Dausner

INTRODUCTION

On 8 December 1965, the Second Vatican Council solemnly concluded, yet fifty years later its reception is far from complete. It now enters a new phase. Until the election of Pope Francis in 2013 the discussion of the hermeneutics of the body of the conciliar texts was in full swing. The question of the authority of the Pastoral Council was a very low priority for some individual interpreters, and the spirit of the Council was variously described. The numerous national and international theological conferences and publications in the years 2012–2015 showed clearly that the Second Vatican Council has been understood by the overwhelming majority of theologians as an epochal event in the church, as a gift of the Spirit. In the past fifty years, however, political, societal, economic, technical, and other changes and processes have occurred that the Council could not have foreseen. Consequently, theology and the church are challenged today to extend the basic theological lines of the Second Vatican Council and in this context to look for future direction.

The title of the International Congress, which took place at the Catholic Academy of Bavaria at the very end of the fiftieth anniversary period from 6 to 8 December 2015, needs to be understood in this connection: "'Disclosing' the Council," the title of the congress, sounds provocative and contentious. The congress did not set out to open up a comprehensive review of the body of texts of the Second Vatican Council in an entirely new way or to discover new aspects in any commentaries of the Council. The "disclosing" was understood to be forward-looking, and this in two respects.

On the one hand, the Second Vatican Council gave theology and the church leadership tasks that have indeed been addressed during the past fifty years but can in no way be regarded as accomplished to the full extent. For example, the following issues are still discussed in a controversial manner:

- How do the Universal Church and the local churches relate to each other, and what implications follow from this for the theological status of national bishops' conferences?
- How can the primacy of the Catholic Church that was taught at the First Vatican Council be integrated into a communio-ecclesiology, and what ecumenical opportunities and implications arise as a result?
- What is the theological relationship of the Catholic Church to non-Christian religions?
- What are the potential opportunities for the dialogical understanding of revelation for a contextual theology?

The list could go on. All these questions were raised by the Council itself. Today, however, issues have arisen as a result of the discussions during the past fifty years of the Council's work as well as from those changes, events, and processes that the Council could not have foreseen.

On the other hand, the Council had for the first time opened itself up to a number of realities that had previously not been seriously considered. It opened itself up, for example, to the modern world and sought a dialogue with it. It was receptive to the ecumenical movement and acknowledged it. It appeared open-minded to non-Christian religions, acknowledging and valuing them theologically and seeking an exchange with them. It took on the legacy of the European Enlightenment and wrote a Declaration on Religious Liberty (*Dignitatis humanae*). These manifold openings issued in programs. As a result of the experience gained since the Council, however, and of the changed historical conditions of today, the following questions arise amongst others:

- What are the consequences of confessing religious liberty and freedom of conscience for the church's understanding

Introduction

of freedom and for the church's structures and its relationship to the modern culture of freedom?
- Starting from the commitment to the prophetic mission of the whole people of God and the sense of faith of all believers, to what extent do synodal and collegial structures belong to ecclesial life so that the involvement and participation of all are guaranteed?
- How is the increasing social, ideological, and religious pluralism, which often degenerates into divisiveness and readiness for violence, to be addressed theologically in the dialogue with the world as well as with non-Christian religions?
- What does the conciliar admission of a certain autonomy of science mean for theology and its relationship to the teaching office of the church?

Again, the list of questions could be extended without any difficulty.

The basic question of the congress, therefore, was: What challenges are on the agenda for theology and the church in the twenty-first century when they consciously seek discourse with contemporary society and want to become aware of their responsibility for shaping the future? The subtitle of the congress expresses this fundamental issue succinctly: "Theology and Church under the Claim of the Second Vatican Council." Thus, the Council statements are taken for granted as a reference point for current and future scientific work, but the programmatic and reformist impulses are further extended. This approach will be important in working toward the next Council.

The mode of operation corresponded to the theme and objective of the congress, To begin with, there was a plenary session with two keynote speeches and two replies to the topic: "On the International Position of the Reception of the Council: Stocktaking and Future Perspectives." This was followed by twelve working groups offering two to four introductory abridged versions of thoroughly prepared papers and a subsequent focused discussion. The presentation of the results was carried out in the form of posters, oral explanations, and brief summaries. The presentation of the groups' findings was followed by an engaged and critical discussion in a plenary session. It formed the basis for the *Declaration of the Congress*, which, again, was critically discussed before being adopted in a plenary session.[1] In this long process of formulating the findings, a public international panel discussion took place during which Cardinal Karl Lehmann gave an opening address. After a Pontifical Mass with Cardinal Reinhard Marx, a multigenerational debate on the Second Vatican Council concluded the congress.

Fortunately it was possible to include representatives from all theological disciplines to collaborate and participate in order to explore the relevance of the Council in the present context of reception on an interdisciplinary level. In addition, numerous Council researchers from other language areas were invited as speakers. Their respective perspectives on the Council of a world church helped to widen the horizon.

Opening Plenary Session on the International Position of the Council's Reception

As already indicated, the congress was opened by a plenary session in which the insights of previous hermeneutical explorations of the conciliar documents and the international status of the reception of the Council were debated and discussed.[2]

Massimo Faggioli, church historian and director of the University of St. Thomas (Saint Paul, Minnesota), characterized the new

---

[1]. All papers read at the Congress and the contributions in the plenary sessions have been published in Christoph Böttigheimer and René Dausner, eds., *Vaticanum 21: Die bleibenden Aufgaben des Zweiten Vatikinischen Konzils im 21. Jahrhundert. Dokumentationsband zum Münchner Kongress "Das Konzil, 'eröffnen'"* (Freiburg i. Br.: Crossroad / Herder & Herder, 2016).

[2]. The two *plenary* sessions are discussed here in more detail so as to provide, together with the publication of the Final Declaration and its commentary in the main part of this book, a first comprehensive overview of the congress.

phase in the reception of the Second Vatican Council according to the work of the current pope, who understands "the Second Vatican Council not as a matter that can be re-interpreted or limited, but as one that should be fulfilled and expanded." In this context Faggioli referred to issues such as collegiality and synodality, which he assessed as "key elements for further developments." He emphasized two elements that are typical of Pope Francis's relationship to the Second Vatican Council: (1) "Francis's access to the Council does not attempt to repair what went wrong at Vatican II or in the postconciliar period nor pay any attention to what had been ignored, forgotten, or omitted from the Second Vatican Council. It deals with the method of the Second Vatican Council as a method for the church of today. Francis makes clear that the theological approach at the Council—attention to the history, the assessment of experience, the inductive method, and the pastoral nature of doctrine—must not be abandoned." (2) Francis is the first pope of a global church. "The election of Jorge Mario Bergoglio is a key moment in the history of the postconciliar church toward the globalization of Catholicism—not only in terms of the internationalization of his Roman collaborators but especially in terms of the ability to inculturate Catholicism into cultures other than those existing in Europe." Therefore, for Faggioli, two challenges and two concrete perspectives of theological work seem to be emerging. On the one hand, Vatican II is to be understood not as a theoretical "pattern" (paradigm) for theology but as a way of acting from which the specific task to appropriate *Gaudium et spes* (the Pastoral Constitution on the Church in the Modern World) emerges in a new way. On the other hand, the "pastoral, acting" ecclesiology of the Second Vatican Council left the Church as an institution virtually untouched, which is why the concrete task of an institutional reform of the church through the rediscovery of the "catholicity of 'development'" (John Henry Cardinal Newman) stands in need of a global perspective.

The Jesuit theologian Christoph Theobald, who teaches at the Centre Sèvres, supplemented and confirmed Faggioli's thesis of the epochal new view of the Council. But while Faggioli developed this view from the program of Jorge Bergoglio as pope, Theobald started from a meta-reflection on Vatican II and the much-changed cultural and geopolitical constellation of church and society since the 1990s. "The Second Vatican Council understands human dignity (*dignitas humana*) as a common ground for church and society and articulates all its questions before this anthropological-ethical background, above all the question of the faith and its ecclesial character or its absence in atheistic humanism." But especially since the fall of the Berlin Wall in 1989 no integral humanism could be assumed anymore, since there is "a radical cultural pluralism and the relativity of all our beliefs, pragmatisms, and probabilities" has taken the place of the still relatively homogeneous worldview of the Council texts.... The fragmentation of our life stories is accompanied by the revival of old and new myths and a kind of neo-Darwinism, which emphasizes the survival of the strongest in finance, politics, and many other areas of society.... With this change of situation we have left behind the cultural horizon of Vatican II." In this pluralistic world there is faith to be professed and proclaimed. There is "an insoluble bond between faith and the validity of everyone's interpretation.... There can be continuing developments only if the basic ethical conditions of any communication—symmetry of the partners, distinction between internal and external perspectives—and, especially in the dialogue with Judaism and other religions, if such symmetry *and* the Christological and eschatological claim of Christianity are brought together."

Given the new constellation, the crucial insight of the Council is its "pastoral nature." "It is rooted in the *modus agendi Christi* (*Dignitatis humanae* [DH] 11), its *modus conversationis* (*Dei Verbum* [DV] 7) and its...poverty and humility (*Lumen gentium* [LG] 8)." The pastoral emphasis allows, "in spite of the completed revelation to include the historical contexts in their interpretation and vice versa to remove from the Word of God principles for the interpretation of the current situation of humankind." This presupposes that the traditional doctrine of faith itself would get to the bottom of its cultural and historical conditions of possibility. All four Constitutions of the Council had made this revision tentatively and in a very initial manner. Would in this given situation the *modus procedendi Iesu* itself be accepted and with it the "pastoral nature" of the Council become the guideline? Then as a maximum, a mutual understanding of synod on equal terms would result. This situation is informed by a messianic vision, "which recalls a perspective of peace for a humanity dominated by violence, as a whole, and opens up the pneumatic sensitivity in the inner life of the churches toward the coming rule of God here and now. It is crucial that the individual problems of daily structural change, often isolated in the reception—from episcopal and particular church collegiality up to the ordination of women and gender issues—will continue to be discussed synodally against the horizon of this messianic eschatological vision." That includes listening to those in [human] societies who have no right to vote.

In answer to these two Council interpretations Emeritus Dogmatist Peter Hünermann from Tübingen first referred to the work during the Council Jubilee 2012–2015 as a time of a comprehensive international theological communication process with respect to the overall interpretation of the Council. Pope Benedict XVI, in his speech to the Roman clergy on 17 February 2013 at the end of his pontificate, stated, "There was the Council of the Fathers—the true Council—but there was also the Council of the media.... The Council, which reached the people with immediate effect, was the one of the media, not the one of the Fathers." The findings of many large theological conferences during these years can, however, be summarized with the insight of Shaji Kotchuthara, the president of the large International Symposium for Asia in Bangalore: The Council "has become the face of the Church, not only for the members of the Church, but also for others."

To complement the two approaches offered in the papers by Faggioli and Theobald, through which the Council needs to be implemented, Hünermann added a third: the all-encompassing social concept of life, in which modern humanity exists with science, technology, and organization, has become the decisive factor of change on the planet earth. The keyword for this change is *anthropocene*. It is this historical parenthesis that embraces the given plurality and polarity of the cultures, the relativity and the antagonism of traditional beliefs, the power-political pragmatism involved and its probabilities and that which forces them toward each other. The faith in God and the hope of salvation in Jesus Christ require in this context a new contemporary shape if the gospel is to be adequately proclaimed today. This new form of faith was only hinted at in the Council; it was not developed. There is no constitution on the faith, not a word about how faith occurs in contemporary everyday human life, and how it would be conceived. The practice of Jesus, his care of the poor, and the approaches of the Pastoral Council needed a new language and pragmatism, which will be formed only as it is implemented. This conclusion would cohere with the findings of Faggioli and Theobald.

Eva-Maria Faber, who teaches dogmatics and fundamental theology at the Theological College in Chur (Switzerland), began her response by asserting, "The Congress, we now hold...at the end of 2015, differs fundamentally from meetings that we could have organized around 2012 at the beginning of this 50th Council anniversary. Thanks are due to Faggioli and Theobald, who clearly demonstrated in their presentations how our academic debate on Vatican II is completely molded by the situation of the contemporary church." The important addition of the Swiss theologian referred to the lack of implementation of a declaration of intent of the Second Vatican Council by the church governing bodies. "The Council established a certain 'way of proceeding,' to which not enough 'practical effort' followed." She mentioned the dispute over the "*subsistit*" (Lumen gentium [LG] 8) as an example of "blocking" the reception of the Council. "In the past, defenders and promoters of the Second Vatican Council had to deal with meeting the forces critical of the Council; Vatican II was the beginning of a beginning, but lacked a continuation so much so that at least the beginning had to be retained with such great vehemence that it

Introduction

was difficult to also identify the shortcomings of the beginning." This led Faber to two "significant desiderata": "To further develop the theory of a teaching office that is not only pastoral but is also provisional. It would need to speak of an authoritativeness, which has to be left behind because of the adopted way of proceeding, so that it will not be counteractive. How strong the myth of an unchanging doctrine of the church is became clear at the last Synod of Bishops." The second desideratum is a more open relationship of the pope and bishops to the "theologians at the periphery" and the recognition of the "freedom of research."

Twelve Workshops

With this prelude, a common reference point was created for the subsequent twelve workshops. While their topics were broadly diversified, their objectives were uniform: to elaborate theological perspectives proceeding from the theological impulses of Vatican II and to identify connecting research objectives. See the documentation of the workshops below.

Public Panel Discussion: "The Council—A New Beginning" (Karl Rahner)

The concluding panel discussion, which was public in contrast to the opening plenary session, was introduced by a masterful shorter address by Cardinal Lehmann. In broad brushstrokes he sketched the "bad defensive position" of the church in the nineteenth and twentieth centuries. The church was "mentally cut off from many living processes"; at the same time, however, there were beginning "reform movements with theological, liturgical, pastoral orientation." The announcement of a Council—"a thunderbolt"—had marked, according to Pope John XXIII., the "boundary line into a new era": "The Pope deliberately wanted the transition from a post-

Tridentine epoch, and to some extent also from the centuries-old Constantinian period, into a new phase of witness and preaching."

The cardinal recalled the efforts paring down the seventy-two topics to be discussed to the sixteen binding documents and characterized in ingenious ways the four Constitutions of the Council on the basis of a postage stamp of "Deutsche Post" from 2012. The stamp depicted *Sacrosanctum concilium* and *Dei Verbum* at the root of the cross and *Lumen gentium* and *Gaudium et spes* on the crossbeams. The understanding of the church is seen in the relation of the four major texts to one another. It is not its own independently defined quantity but, as the sacrament of salvation in the world, is "directed toward the Triune God, who descends to us and at the same time reaches to humankind all over the whole world and to all oppressed (Option for the poor, Treaty of the Catacombs)."

Regarding the impact of the Council, Lehmann listed briefly aspects of the "transformation of Catholicism on the Central and South American subcontinent," the "innumerable ecumenical documents in bilateral and multilateral dialogues," and the "dialogue with Judaism and the non-Christian religions." He mentioned an area with which the church still has difficulties. In his opinion, it is "the greatest break in the common social conditions of the past fifty years": the lessening of a certain self-understanding of speech about God, the languishing of the sensitivity for something like transcendence "and in contrast to it an ever greater, almost boundless autonomy and freedom"—in brief, "the loss of the dimension of the Holy." For him, the main future prospects were the synodality of the church and its fundamental missionary character.

The subsequent statements related to:

- The global networking of theologians in the face of questions posed all over the world. This was illustrated by James Keenan, SJ (Boston, Massachusetts, USA), on the basis of the global network of moral theologians and social ethicists.

Introduction

- The Universal Church character of the Catholic Church. From her long experience as a Catholic consultant at the World Council of Churches and her academic activities in Leuven, Anne Marie Mayer (University of Leuven, Belgium) spoke of the self-perception of the Catholic Church as a global church and of the implied question of "churches with subjective character" within the global church and the "most urgent pastoral questions on a world level" such as the "ecumenism of the martyrs" as a new paradigm of ecumenism.
- The reception of the Council. Massimo Faggioli emphatically outlined the reception of the Council in the theology of the church, the preaching of the church, and the church's involvement in politics in the United States. He elucidated the difficult relation between discourse that is politically motivated and at the same time social, including religious views and the differentiating ecclesial doctrine of faith.
- The *teología india*. Bernadetta Coero Bustillos, Old Testament scholar at Theological Institute San Pablo (Cochabamba, Bolivia), depicted this new type of theology as the most recent blossom of the Council, eventful and vibrant.
- Pursuing the traditional concept. Christoph Theobald clarified the need to start from *Dei Verbum* and *Nostra aetate* (NA). Even the revelation claim of Christianity needs to be articulated anew.

The "Finale" of the Congress

The "finale" of the congress was marked by two events. The first was the solemn and common celebration of the Eucharist, presided over by Cardinal Marx, who interpreted the Council as gift of God's Spirit to guide the people of God, the church in our times. The second event was the final discussion and the fairly unanimous approval of a joint declaration, which was published immediately.

The stated aim of this final declaration is to reflect on the theological and ecclesial insights of the Twenty-First Ecumenical Council in the changed political, economic, and sociological—and not least, the religious—conditions of the twenty-first century and to think ahead as "theology and the church under the claim of the Second Vatican Council."

The busy congress concluded with a relaxed multigenerational debate. Next to emeritus and eyewitness of the Council Professor Josef Wohlmuth (Bonn) was seated university lecturer René Dausner from Eichstätt. On the podium also were two younger theologians, Dr. Regina Heyder and Dr. Judith Samson, both academic staff in research projects relating to the Council. They all talked about the encounter with the Council, which, in very different situations, was a powerful incentive for their theological development and their works and projects. These moving accounts reminded the participants of the congress of their own history: the Council as *dynamis pneumatikē*, opening completely new dimensions and making tangible painful limits.

Four days after the solemn closing of Vatican II, on 12 December 1965, Karl Rahner said at a ceremony in the Munich Herkulessaal: "Of course, it will take a long time until the Church, which was offered a Second Vatican Council by God, will become the Church of the Second Vatican Council." The aim of this congress was to contribute to this conciliar renewal and implementation process under the claim of the Second Vatican Council.

Finally thanks were offered to the Catholic Academy of Bavaria, which collaborated as a partner in the congress. In addition, gratitude was expressed to the German Research Foundation (Deutsche Forschungsgesellschaft), which, together with the Cassianeum Foundation and the German Bishops' Conference, promoted and supported the project financially. Appreciation was also extended to Cardinal Reinhard Marx, who actively supported the organization of the International Congress in Munich as well as to Cardinal Karl Lehmann, who was the Honorary President of the Congress.

Christoph Böttigheimer
Chairman of the Congress Bureau

BUREAU MEMBERS:

Prof. Dr. Franz Xaver Bischof, Munich
PD Dr. René Dausner, Eichstatt
Prof. Dr. Marianne Heimbach-Steins, Münster
Prof. em. Dr. Peter Hünermann, Tübingen
Prof. Dr. Benedikt Kranemann, Erfurt
Prof. Dr. Johanna Rahner, Tübingen
Prof. Dr. Joachim Schmiedl, Vallendar
Prof. em. Dr. Josef Wohlmuth, Bonn

FINAL DECLARATION OF THE INTERNATIONAL CONGRESS: "'DISCLOSING' THE COUNCIL"

6–8 December 2015 at the Catholic Academy of Bavaria, Munich

On the fiftieth anniversary of the solemn closing of the Second Vatican Council, some two hundred theologians gathered from 6 to 8 December 2015 for an International Congress in Munich. Their concern was to reflect on the impulses of the Council regarding the tasks of German Catholic theology in the twenty-first century and to think further ahead. Theology sees itself in a special way challenged to interpret the signs of the times: it thereby follows the Council's mode of operation, given by Pope John XXIII, to bear witness to the gospel in a pastoral way responding to the joys and hardships of the people today: to be theology in the service of humankind and the contemporary world (*aggiornamento*).

1. Freedom and Faith

In recognizing religious liberty as a human right, the Second Vatican Council for the first time takes the claim to liberty of modernity positively. But as long as freedom of conscience, freedom of opinion, and the rights of the participation of the faithful are not fully recognized in the church, the nature of faith as an act of freedom is only incompletely taken into account. Human rights, based on the dignity of the human being, must be implemented within the church for the sake of the church's credibility. Theology is faced with the task of articulating concerns about freedom from the center of its understanding of faith for the church's life and for the global social and political reality and to argue for its realization in concrete contexts. To understand the faith as the fulfilment of freedom, as a scientific form of reflecting the faith, requires that theology can claim this necessary freedom.

We are committed to taking seriously the conditional relationship between faith and freedom. In today's global conditions this demands that we look for alliances comprising denominations, religions, and ideologies in favor of free conditions of life, among other things, to search for religious liberty and freedom of conscience, and to vigorously carry them forward. Theology herewith takes part in the responsibility of the church to the world.

2. Theology as a Science

The Council has been prepared by theological developments of the early twentieth century and has set central impulses even for theology. Theology is understood in the sense of tradition alongside the teaching office of the bishops as an indispensable scientific teaching authority in the church and as an important space of understanding-oriented discourse in the public sphere.

We are committed to looking, for the sake of a deeper knowledge of the truth, for interdisciplinary debate with all sciences as well as exchange with the wisdom traditions of different cultures and the lived practice of faith. For this, theology itself must make efforts to clarify its self-understanding as a science and to provide for an intensive exchange between its individual branches.

3. Theology and the Episcopal Teaching Office

The Second Vatican Council has in a model way implemented the task of the pastorally understood teaching office of the bishops to moderate the interpretation process of tradition and the experience of faith. In this process, which implies self-relativization, including the courage of revising doctrinal statements, theology plays an important role. The congress is recommending that those responsible in the church attach particular importance to theological science, especially in view of today's educational societies. Despite recurrent and inevitable tensions in the relationship between the theological and episcopal teaching office, the discourse about the interpretation of faith needs to be open-ended. Only in this way can the freedom of theology be guaranteed as a science. In particular, it must be a concern of the church in this context to promote scientific theology at state universities.

We are committed to further developing such a process along the lines of the Second Vatican Council. Care must in the future be taken so that the people of God shall be free to speak in their many voices.

4. Reform of Ecclesial Structures

The Council finds a renewed self-conception of the church by, among other things, moving back to the center the image of the church as the people of God as well as by collegiality and by engaging in a human rights–oriented hermeneutics. Theology has to work toward overcoming the tensions between the hierarchical and communal ecclesiology of the Second Vatican Council in returning to the dialogical understanding of revelation in *Dei Verbum*. Synodality needs to become again a structural principle in the church. It is the consequence of a pneumatological ecclesiology and finds expression in the discernment of minds. It must be legally implemented and be enforceable; it also needs to be studied at all levels of the church.

We are committed to assisting in the development of a synodal church structure. The much-needed reform of the Roman Curia, which is sought, must lead to a reform of the entire church and the church's ministry. Important decisions of the church that claim public validity must not be made behind closed doors. "What concerns all, should also be dealt with by all" recalled Pope Francis in his address of 17 October 2015 on the issue of the synodality in the church.

5. Inner-Christian Ecumenism

The Council has made possible amazing ecumenical developments; at the same time divergent trends need to be observed in retrospect: The Catholic Church has opened itself to the ecumenical movement and established dialogues with other churches, after abandoning its exclusivistic self-understanding. The "Joint Declaration on the Doctrine of Justification" is the highlight of this development. For many believers, the ecumenical being together has become normal. The awareness has grown and been accepted that it is not unity that needs to be justified, but it is the maintenance of division that does. There are, however, expressions of the church leadership that seem to imply a return to an outdated understanding of the church; many Catholics no longer suffer from the situation of division but see it as a given factor; confessional and denominational differences no longer play such a significant role.

We are committed to promoting methodical reflection in ecumenical dialogue and ecumenical pastoral practice. Important topics for further work include, among others, criteria for church fellowship and its limitations; expression of the ecumenical opening in other ecclesiastical features such as liturgy or canon law; and the development of models of unity, which are not found in the Council documents.

6. The Church and Judaism

The Council made groundbreaking basic statements on the relationship between the church and Judaism. The congress fully affirms the directives and the findings of earlier Christian–Jewish conversations. In view of the guilt arising from history in church and theology, this remains a permanent commitment.

We are committed to respecting this obligation in all theological disciplines and to receiving it more deeply. When translating and interpreting biblical and liturgical texts, we are committed to bearing in mind the Jewish context and to avoiding all forms of anti-Judaism. In society, theology speaks out against any kind of anti-Semitism and xenophobia. In the indispensable dialogue between Christianity and Islam, theology advocates maintaining the unique relationship between Jews and Christians as the basis of the Christian–Muslim dialogue.

7. The Claim of Revelation and the Plurality of Religions

The Council teaches the theological understanding of revelation as the self-mediation of God. For the relevant texts, however, a profound clarification of the philosophical implications is still lacking, on which the connection to secular discourses can be ensured. In addition, an adequate reading of these texts needs to take into consideration the highly differentiated reception processes on the international level.

We are committed to exploring interreligious differences in the concept of revelation and to deepening the religious and traditional concepts. This will lead to a fundamental redefinition of dogmatics and fundamental theology. The relationship between revelation and religions has to be widened to include the dimension of respect for humanity with the question of the religious existence of self at its center.

8. Interreligious Dialogue and Mission

The Council values non-Christian religions and pleads for interreligious dialogue. How this can succeed on equal terms has not been fully discussed in postconciliar theology. The congress sees this as an important theological task for the future. Moreover, it opposes any kind of fundamentalism and religious self-isolation.

We are committed to practicing and promoting unbiased and discursive relations with other religions. Although we appreciate the achievements of missionaries in preaching and in the social and educational spheres, we must consistently reappraise the history of guilt, which has been caused by mission and colonization in the past centuries. Mission belongs to the essence of the church; it is the reciprocal communication of the gospel and manifests itself in diaconia, the option for the poor, and dialogue with cultures and religions.

9. Liturgy and Inculturation

The Council has launched a comprehensive reform of the liturgy. The congress values the result of this reform for the life of faith and the participation of the faithful. It advocates its continuation with the strong participation of the local churches. A living liturgy requires an ongoing reflection thanks to an inculturated theology, which must be developed in dialogue with the cultural and social sciences. The congress discerns the unity of the Catholic Church and the diversity of rites as an opportunity for a dynamic faith.

We are committed to exploring the rich history of liturgies expressing the faith in the local churches of all continents. At the present time, we are particularly challenged by the changed realities of religiously shaped cultures, confessionalism, and atheism.

10. Faith and Formation/Education

The Council sees the theological formation of the faithful as a central task of the church. This applies to both the laity and the clergy alike. For the congress, religious formation belongs to the enlightened educational norm of secular society. Considering constitutional conditions all religious communities must be allowed the opportunity to undertake educational work that promotes the autonomy of the subject and affects positively the integration process in a pluralistic society.

We are committed to demonstrating the indispensability of obvious, religious resources for the discourse of civil society and to promoting religious education/formation, which will serve to answer the question of meaning in a free society, without wanting to dominate it.

11. *The Church and the Media*

In the Council, the church entered in a new way into the debate with secular society. The urgency of this debate has since sharpened dramatically. About fifty years ago, the Council Fathers could not have imagined the breakthrough to a technology-based, digital information and communication society. Church and theology need to be open to this technological and social change, to try to help shape it productively as well as critically, and to develop specific forms of media communication for passing on the faith.

We are committed to theologically better penetrating the dynamics of media reality, to making it pastorally fruitful, to intensifying dialogue with the secular public, and to activating the inner-ecclesial and theological opinion-forming process and position training more than before.

12. *Creation and Ecology*

The Council welcomes the extension of human dominion over earthly creation but at the same time makes clear that the human being is part of nature and, as an image of God, needs to behave responsibly toward nonhuman nature. The ecological and social crisis that is currently beginning to assume catastrophic proportions has been acknowledged in its full range only since the end of the

1960s. In the Anthropocene, humanity has become a fateful power for the entire biosphere. On the world social level, a number of lost balances need to be restored: between state and market, between the individual and society, between women and men, between short- and long-term thinking, and between slowness and acceleration.

We are committed to placing the integrity of creation and environmental issues at the center of theological work. Theology is challenged to enter into an intensive exchange with the natural sciences and to distance itself from ideological one-sidedness (secularist naturalism and fundamentalist creationism). In this process it has to articulate anew the basic concepts of its doctrine of creation. A rich potential can be found, for instance, in Christian wisdom traditions and indigenous theologies. Theology can and must support the urgently needed transformation processes toward "sustainability."

This joint final declaration was adopted on 7 December 2015. Fifty years ago, the reciprocal excommunication between East and West was lifted. On the same day the Pastoral Constitution *Gaudium et spes* and the Declaration on Religious Liberty *Dignitatis humanae* were adopted as the last documents of the Second Vatican Council.

In memory of these events and in conjunction with theologians from other parts of the global church, theology has the obligation to prioritize the unity of the churches and the dialogue of religions, the defense of the dignity and the rights of all people, and the integrity of the whole creation. Our God-talk in the twenty-first century has to be tested by engaging in these concerns.

> Responsible for this declaration is the Congress Bureau.
> Munich, 8 December 2015
>
> Cardinal Karl Lehmann, Honorary President
>
> Prof. Dr. Franz Xaver Bischof, Munich
> Prof. Dr. Christoph Böttigheimer, Eichstatt
> PD Dr. René Dausner, Eichstatt

Prof. Dr. Marianne Heimbach-Steins, Münster
Prof. em. Dr. Peter Hünermann, Tübingen
Prof. Dr. Benedikt Kranemann, Erfurt
Prof. Dr. Johanna Rahner, Tübingen
Prof. Dr. Joachim Schmiedl, Vallendar
Prof. em. Dr. Josef Wohlmuth, Bonn

DOCUMENTATION OF THE TWELVE WORKSHOPS

1. Freedom and Faith

MEMBERS OF THE PREPARATION TEAM

Prof. Dr. Marianne Heimbach-Steins, Münster
Prof. Dr. Saskia Wendel, Cologne
Prof. Dr. Stephan Goertz, Mainz

INTERNATIONAL CONSULTANTS

Prof. Dr. Georg Essen, Bochum
  "... *Our contemporaries make much of this freedom and pursue it eagerly" (GS 17). Notes on the Relationship of Catholicism and Freedom*
Prof. Dr. James Keenan, SJ, Boston
  Collective Conscience and Collective Guilt

COMMENTARY: *Marianne Heimbach-Steins, Saskia Wendel*

"Freedom" is a key anthropological, ethical, and practical-political category of the modern age. Each individual human person is to be granted the status as a subject and a person. The definition of the human person as a being of freedom is closely connected with this status. Freedom means not only the negative freedom from constraint and alien definition but also the positive freedom for the development of potential as a subject and a person, for creativity and the capacity for a new beginning. Freedom is freedom of will and decision. It is at the same time the potential condition for morality.

Freedom establishes the principles of a moral and legal order that corresponds to the moral self-affirmation of the person. At the same time it standardizes alongside justice and solidarity the relations of recognition of the socialized subject. Because of this background, the definition of the relation of freedom and morality, of freedom and power, as well as of freedom and institutions, becomes the central task of anthropology, ethics, and political theory.

This understanding of freedom characterizes the theological understanding of faith in modern societies and forms the standard for its institutional fulfillment, that is, for the appearance of the church. Christian faith is free assent to the self-revealing God. Moreover, human freedom is indebted in a trusting perspective to God, the Creator. It is the fundamental characteristic of the divine likeness. If freedom really belongs to the divine likeness, then the same is valid for faith. This is valid for the relation of freedom and restriction, and thus also for the aspect of autonomy of faith. Because Christian faith is lived in the midst of society and also in institutional ways, the same standard in the determination of freedom and power as well as freedom and institutions must be established in the church as in society.

The Second Vatican Council has supported this insight with the recognition of human rights as the right of freedom in society, especially along with the recognition of the freedom of religion as the right of the person. Thus, the Council has taken leave programmatically of the anti-modernism of the past. But the church can externally intercede only authentically for the recognition and realization of the right of freedom of all persons, independently of ethnicity, social origin, and gender, if it recognizes this right for itself in its social form. In view of the right of freedom *ad intra*, the relation of freedom and restraint stands here at the center according to the foundation and legitimation of traditional ecclesial orders and institutions. Moreover, this relation needs a reflection theologically about the understanding of faith as an act of positive and negative freedom, of a deepened ecclesiological foundation of the church as sign and instrument of God's freedom and of human freedom and of a corresponding formation of its order.

Paradigmatically for the indicated tension, there is beyond the question of the freedom of individual conscience the freedom of religion. Since the late 1960s freedom of conscience has been used frequently within the church as the legitimation of dissension to magisterial positions. From the perspective of the teaching office, the appeal to freedom of conscience was valid often as an expression of a merely subjective morality. It is a central theological-ethical task to ask according to which criteria a certain case is determined. What designates a correctly formed conscience and what latitudes of freedom are allowed for proper decisions of conscience, in what contexts of life?

The Catholic Church is challenged to find in a culture of freedom a trustworthy form for the Christian faith. This includes the task, *ad extra* to accompany critically the process of freedom in society and to react to its ambivalence without declining into a cultural pessimism skeptical of freedom. Even if the origin of the understanding of freedom outlined here lies in Western culture and society, its claim of validity is universal in spite of this particular genesis. Accordingly, it is also the task of the global church, without prejudice to cultural differences and material characteristics, to recognize internally and externally completely the right of freedom as an analogue to human rights. If this task is successful, then the church worldwide will have arrived, where the Council fifty years before had made a start: in the modern world.

2. *Theology as a Science*

MEMBERS OF THE PREPARATION TEAM

Prof. Dr. Gerhard Kruip, Mainz
Prof. Dr. Alexander Loichinger

INTERNATIONAL CONSULTANTS

Prof. Dr. Christa Schnabel, Vienna
On the Importance of Theology/Theologies in Public Universities: Reflections from the Perspective of a University Administration

Prof. Dr. Claus Arnold, Mainz
Theology as a Science: Comments of a Church Historian

Prof. Dr. Michael Schramm, Hohenheim
Theology as Science

Prof. Dr. Alexander Loichinger, Mainz
Theology as Science in Interdisciplinary Exchange

COMMENTARY: *Gerhard Kruip/Alexander Loichinger*

According to Anselm of Canterbury (1033–1109) faith seeks its own understanding (*fides quaerens intellectum*). Already in the Old and New Testaments there is reference to this, that the human person as a reason-gifted being seeks to make her/his faith for him-/herself plausible in relation to others (see 1 Peter 3:15). Therefore, there are already theologies in the Bible. The Apologists sought to formulate the central content of their faith with the resources of the ancient philosophies of that time. They even understood Christian faith as the better philosophy. Thomas Aquinas (1225–1274) made Aristotle, the most recent philosophical theory of his time, the foundation of his theological reflection. In the tradition of Thomas, Catholic theology even today understands itself as the "essential teaching office in the church."

In the Pastoral Constitution *Gaudium et spes* of the Second Vatican Council, the increasing importance of sciences in society is positively accepted (GS 5, 7, 15, 33, 44, 52, 54, and repeated), and a certain autonomy is granted to them (GS 36, 59). Accordingly, the Council demands of theology that it cooperate closely with other sciences, certainly in the adherence to its proper method (GS 62).

With this background of close and mutual reference of faith and reason, it is not surprising that the establishment of the first universities from the eleventh to thirteenth centuries started with ecclesial authorities, and the theological faculties inside the "house of sciences" formed the first of the faculties. From a historical point of view theology has significantly shaped the idea of occidental science. The foregone conclusions of the university arrangement of theology have severely been shaken since the Enlightenment, with the functional differentiation of modern sciences and the emancipation of ecclesial and civil authorities. The prioritizing of empirical research, the repression of speculative positions, the limitation of falsifiable hypotheses, as well as the affirmation of a freedom of presuppositions and value, today decisively characterize the modern ideal of science. Theology by its very nature cannot be in accord in all areas. Where these criteria are applied in an inappropriate way overall to all sciences, sciences of another spirit also get involved. Indeed also the human and social sciences are under a pressure similar to that on theology. To most colleagues (women and men) of other faculties confession-bound theology appears as the possibility of interference of ecclesial authorities as foreign bodies in the contemporary university.

In this situation, it is very welcome that the German Council of Science (der Deutsche Wissenschaftsrat) has spoken out clearly in a recommendation of 29 January 2010 that theologies—including Islamic theology— are permitted and should have a legitimate place in the universities: a scholarly reflection of religion is of great worth not only for concerned believers but for society as a whole. By means of scholarly theology believers can be put in a position in a post-secular time to introduce their convictions, approached from faith, in open conversation and in democratic processes of decision making. This could involve relevant ethical questions and questions of the common welfare. It would be valuable for society if religions made accessible their resources, given meaning by tradition, in a discussion open to those who are not believers, for their own existential search for meaning. Finally, scholarly-theological reflection on the relativization of one's own traditions could contribute to the avoidance of fundamentalism, to a better understanding of global sites of conflict, and to a more intensive interreligious and intercultural exchange, which our present society so pressingly needs. At the same time, the Council of Science recommended the withdrawal of ecclesial authorities from the process of habilitations.

In the theology of the modern age, the differentiation of various theological subjects has arisen, which in a certain way take up the spectrum of university disciplines. The scholarly understanding of theological subjects has an influence through the nontheological sciences on relative sciences: church history by the science of history, biblical subjects by the science of literature, and so on. Many of the claims of validity raised at the same time do not differ from their nontheological relative sciences.

This is valid also for fundamental theology and dogmatics. Fundamental theology works with the theory of science and philosophy; dogmatics, which works hermeneutically in the understanding of its own tradition of faith, which examines ideas of faith for consistency, expresses its formulations in contemporary language and uses therefore distinctive philosophical positions.

All theological subjects stand in a more or less direct reference to these branches of theology. These branches exert a decisive influence on each other and have a claim of validity.

For its inherent task of reflection of faith and the practice of faith to be accomplished, theology is not allowed to decline into its different subjects, but it must work in an interdisciplinary manner and strive constantly in a communicative process for the unity of theology. At the same time theology must also strengthen interdisciplinary cooperation with nontheological subjects. In addition, many other questions belong here, which modern physics, the theory of evolution, or brain-research direct to religious concepts.

Religious communities today stand ever more strongly in a religiously plural context. At the same time there are processes of cultural pluralization in the religious communities themselves. The Catholic Church no longer has its center of gravity in Europe.

Therefore, theology must become involved in the wisdom traditions from other cultures, as it did, for example, in the project of *"teología india"* in Latin America. It may possibly learn something about itself and may thereby regain partially lost spiritual experiences also in Europe.

3. *Theology and the Episcopal Teaching Office*

MEMBERS OF THE PREPARATION TEAM

Prof. Dr. Sabine Demel, Regensburg
Prof. Dr. Christoph Böttigheimer, Eichstätt
PD Dr. René Dausner, Eichstätt

INTERNATIONAL CONSULTANTS

Prof. Dr. Peter Neuner, Munich
The Teaching Office and Theology
Prof. Dr. Jürgen Werbick, Münster
The Freedom of Theology—and Its Ecclesial Reconnection
Prof. Dr. Klaus Unterburger, Regensburg
Infallible Faith, sensus fidei and the Pastoral Teaching Office in Historical Perspective

COMMENTARY: *Christoph Böttigheimer, René Dausner*

The constituting of theology as the science of faith caused Thomas Aquinas to distinguish the teaching office of bishops (*magisterium cathedrae pastoralis*, i.e., *pontificalis*) from the teaching office of the theologians (*magisterium cathedrae magistralis*).[1] Matters of the pastoral teaching office are the handed-on teaching of the faith. Matters of the theological teaching office are the anal-

---

1. Thomas Aquinas, *Quodl.* II, 9 ad 3; *In IV Sent.* ds. 19 qu. 2 ar. 2b ra 4.

ysis of the faith supported by the principles of faith and reason, the proof of their inner coherence. An irreducible independence is the property of both teaching offices. While the pope and bishops are devoted to the function of testifying to the Word of God, theologians are devoted to the scholarly investigation of the ecclesially testified faith.

Because the episcopal office is provided with the power of administration peculiar to it, it is the office of guardian over unity and continuity of the church's faith. It claims the right of the definition of faith (*determinatio fidei*).[2] The independence of theological teaching does not question the episcopal competence of decision making. Nevertheless, on the constructive as well as critical function of university theology, a scientific and pastoral teaching office stands in a polar-tension relation that is analogous to the relation of faith and science.

Theology requires a scientific autonomy—freedom of thought, of methodology, of independent judgment, of scholarly discourse, of open-ended research. It is of its nature related to ecclesially proclaimed faith and is subordinated to the apostolic office with its normative, regulative function.

In the Second Vatican Council, theology gained an enormous importance. The final declaration correctly stated, "The Second Vatican Council has implemented in an exemplary way the task of a pastorally understood teaching office of bishops to present the interpretive process of Tradition and experience of the faith. In this process, which implied a self-relativization, including the courage of revision of magisterial statements, theology plays an important role."

The conciliar texts witness to the importance of theology for culture, mediation of faith, and ecclesial life (GS 44, 62; GE 11). This includes the "just freedom, to engage in research, to reflect, as well as to express its opinion in humility and firmness" (GS 62).

The hierarchical teaching office is referred to the other loci theologici. There is no authority of testimony of the Word of God

---

2. Cf. Thomas Aquinas, *S.Th*. II-II, q. 1, a. 10; q. 11, a. 2 ad 3.

without the others. Especially the infallible totality of the faithful has by right an active role in the authentic preservation of God's Word (LG 12).

The appreciation of theology in the conciliar texts is clouded by unexamined, ecclesial modes of speaking (DV 10; LG 25). At the same time, the question remained open which role in general is by right that of the episcopal office in the context of a communication-theory understanding of revelation and in a dynamic-open process of tradition connected to it. Are not theology and the faithful in the same way involved in the hermeneutical process of faith?

Theology that depended on a dialogical concept of revelation was increasingly repressed in the postconciliar period. Tensions between the episcopal and theological teaching offices increasingly appeared. They ignited ethical questions, contextual theologies, and so on, and led to a renewed marginalization of theology by the ecclesial teaching office.[3] The Council's interrogation of the teaching office and theology was, to a large extent, lost.

If theology as the science of faith is a self-performance of the church, the church by necessity needs an academic-scientific theology. In 1980, Pope John Paul II reaffirmed theological research and teaching. He affirmed that academic theology "in the use of its methods and analysis" be free and that the teaching office and theology "could not be reduced to one another" since both would have to fulfill different tasks.[4] These statements did not lead to any postconciliar revaluation of theological work.

This tendency to marginalize theology gives rise to the question, of how the interaction of the episcopal office, theology, and the *sensus fidei fidelium* can be formed. The final declaration answers,

---

3. See Professio fidei und Lehranmerkungen DH 5070–5072.
4. Johannes Paul II, Ansprache bei Begegnung mit Theologieprofessoren . . . in Altötting am 18 November 1980: Theologie und Kirche. Dokumentation. 31 März 1991. Ed. Sekretariat der Deutschen Bischofskonferenz (= Arbeitshilfen 86, Bonn 1991, 66–71, here 69–70).

"In spite of ever-repeating and necessary tensions in the relation of the theological and episcopal teaching office, the discourse about the interpretation of the faith must be led to open results."

On the basis of differentiated areas of responsibility of the ecclesial teaching office and theological research, the latter must establish an extensive space to reflect as this is applied to the bishops. They will have reflections to be stated that extend beyond the validating norms at this time. This is an absolutely necessary service for the church.

The pastoral teaching office, theology, and the meaning of faith of the believers, which concerns the authority of teaching, are unequal partners. Nevertheless the ecclesial teaching office as a corresponding partial subject has to respect as a full-value dialogue partner theology and the people of God with their sense of the faith: the renewal of the church depends on it (GS 92). A freely critical communication "on the level of equality" (*Unitatis redintegratio* [UR] 9) excludes on the part of the *pastoral* teaching office *judicative* acts, which hinder free discourse or prematurely end it by a demand for obedience. Questions of faith as a rule are endured so long in discourse until a "magnus consensus" is crystallized. Therefore on the part of the teaching office they have to remain open.

4. Reform of Ecclesial Structures

MEMBERS OF THE PREPARATION TEAM

Prof. Dr. Johanna Rahner, Tübingen
Prof. Dr. Gerd Häfner, Munich
Prof. Dr. Franz Xaver Bischof, Munich

INTERNATIONAL CONSULTANTS

Prof. Dr. Bradford E. Hinze, Fordham
  Synodality and Democracy For We Are the People

Prof. Dr. Adrian Loretan, Lucerne
The People of God and Their Order: A contribution to human rights

COMMENTARY: *Franz Xaver Bischof, Gerd Häfner, Johanna Rahner*

Adrian Loretan underlines that the Roman Catholic Church defends human rights globally, and the Council in the declaration *Dignitatis humanae* has founded the constitutional right of each human being on the freedom of religion with human dignity. As a result, the demand that human dignity also must be a basic concept of the ecclesial order again demands basic rights, which are valid for *each* person in the church and, as in every other organization, must be anchored and protected in the ecclesial order. The church at the same time could have recourse to the natural-law intellectual tradition as well as to the modern concept of order.

The chief thesis of Bradford Hinze's lecture about *synodality and democracy* is that the promotion of active participation of the people of God in the church requires different forms of solidarity and democracy, which recognize the existence of conflicts and pathologies in the church and society as well as the role of conflict and debate for consensus-formation. Something identical is valid for the discussion in civil and ecclesial life, and indeed as well in the formation of relationships and also in the continuous striving for common well-being, which includes a diversity of worldviews. Hinze illustrates his thesis (a) in the affinity between synodality in the church and democracy in the civil society of Western character; (b) in the loss of meaning of the people-of-God ecclesiology under the Popes John Paul II (1978–2005) and Benedict XVI (2005–2013). They indeed have confirmed both synodal structures of administration in the local church, but at the same time reduced their effectiveness, as they attributed to them only an adversarial function. This again serves the justification of an office of central authority; (c) in the reform agenda of the present Pope Francis, which represents a new phase of the reception of the Council's teaching by the church as people of God, by *sensus fidelium*, by the signs of the time, and by dialogue as characteristics of a synodal church. A prerequisite for the success of this process would be self-involvement in an open dialogue according to the model of the papacy, which risks a "conflictive consensus" as, on the one hand, part of subject formation and, on the other hand, the transitional being of the church by a formation of common judgment.

The impulse of both lectures leads to further critical inquiries in the course of which three central challenges are found for theology and church.

1. The question of the capacity for conflict in those cultures in which a structure of dialogue and dispute, as it developed in Euro-Atlantic countries, is strange;
2. The question of the natural tension between synodality and authority;
3. The question of the transformation of human rights and democratic participation *in* the church.

These challenges urgently demand in the present phase of the Council's reception a re-updating of pneumatology. Pneumatology until now in the order of the church et al., with its limitation of synodal elements to purely legal advice, has experienced no adequate transformation. On the other hand, a deepened theological and ecclesiological reflection of the declaration *Dignitatis humanae* is fitting, whose inner-church relevance wishes to be circumspect and must have consequences for the hermeneutic of canon law.

As a thematic focal point for the further reception, the following complexes of questions were identified. They are represented in the framework of scholarly reflection of theology, but also for the administrative organs on all ecclesial levels (dioceses, church provinces, episcopal conferences, total church) to the ecclesial legislators as to the people of God in total as the central, future tasks (of research and fields of activity.

The reflection about this, as the juxtaposition of two ecclesiologies, as it is applied in the church constitution *Lumen gentium* (LG 21/22), can be brought into a definition of a fruitful relationship. In addition, a recourse to the content of *Dei Verbum* is fundamental and can be helpful in an understanding of revelation oriented to dialogue and communication and to its ecclesiological implications.

Then synodality, as it is anchored and well established in the ecclesial tradition of the first millennium (*Quod omnes tangit ab omnibus tractari debet / What touches all should be considered an approved by all*) must again become the structural principle of the church. It is an outflow and structure-shaping form of a pneumatological ecclesiology and must not only legally be transformed and be legally recoverable by the institution of an ecclesial court of administration, but it must become concrete and exercised on all levels of church life-practice.

In his address on the occasion of the fiftieth anniversary of the establishment of the Synod of Bishops on 15 October 2015, Pope Francis declared that it would be a goal of his pontificate to re-evaluate the Synod of Bishops as "one of the most precious legacies" of the Council, already only because "the world in which we live and which in all its contradictoriness we are called to love and to serve . . . demands of the church an increase of its collaboration in all areas of its mission." The pope explicitly believes in synodality as the principle of structure of the church when he establishes programmatic items: "Exactly this way of synodality is what God expects from the church of the third millennium."

That the structure of a synodal church will have consequences for the Petrine function and ecumenism is not only wished by the pope but is a necessary requirement that a synodally organized church in the global perspective can also be a model for people and societies living together.

5. Inner-Christian Ecumenism

MEMBERS OF THE PREPARATION TEAM

Prof. Dr. h.c. mult. Peter Hünermann, Tübingen
Prof. Dr. Miriam Wijlens, Erfurt
Prof. Dr. Paul D. Murray, Durham
Prof. Dr. Thomas Bremer, Münster

INTERNATIONAL CONSULTANTS

Prof. Dr. André Birmelé, Strasbourg
On the Status of Present Ecumenical Efforts
Prof. Dr. Paul D. Murray, Durham
Receptive Ecumenism and Reduction
Prof. Dr. Evgeny Pilipenko, Moscow
Dogmatic Thought and Ecumenical Ethos: A Critical Examination of the Problematic Relationship in Orthodoxy
Prof. Dr. Miriam Wijlens, Erfurt
Church and Churches—Institutions of Law in the Process of Growing Unity

COMMENTARY: *Thomas Bremer, Maria Wernsmann*

The consultants and the participants in the panel agree practically on three points:

1. The openness of the Catholic Church to the ecumenical movement and to the strengthening of ecumenism by Protestants among themselves and Orthodox, which resulted from the Second Vatican Council, is surprising. The dialogues fill thousands of pages. Far-reaching results are documented in the four volumes of *Growth in Agreement.*
2. The mutual Catholic/Reformation/Anglican/Orthodox dialogue process, involving the best theological experts,

appears not to reach further results that lead to visible church unity or church fellowship. Statements of the ecclesial teaching office appear to imply a return to outdated understandings of the church. *"Dominus Iesus"* (2000) is an example of this.

The apostolic constitution *Anglicanorum Coetibus* (2009) puts in question the rejection of return-ecumenism, while it created a legal foundation for the acceptance of groups of Anglicans into the Catholic Church. Ecumenical dialogue has no effect on the liturgy or on canon law.

3. The "Joint Declaration on the Doctrine of Justification" (JDDJ) was named universally in the discussion as a high point of ecumenical development.

Paul Murray introduced—from the experience in Catholic/Anglican dialogue, the difficulties and stagnation—"receptive ecumenism." The central question is, What can a church learn for the solution of its own problems from other churches? For Murray this is a way that can yield results. The readiness and the capacity of the church for change are the focuses of the discussion. A conversion of the churches means not a loss of identity but a gain. On this point the participants of the panel were in strong agreement (UR 6–8).

André Birmelé, who participates in the Lutheran–Roman Catholic dialogue, shed light on the inner logic of the numerous dialogues—from Malta onwards—conditioned by the obvious key differences over ecclesiology. He differentiated sharply between the nature of the language of theological experts and the peculiarity of the decisions of church leaders. These decisions are dependent on the theological and church political declarations from church leadership as well as on the reception of the people of God, the believers. Such declarations express an item of faith in different ways and are characterized by the structure of reconciled diversity.[5] This for Birmelé

---

5. See the *Joint Declaration on the Doctrine of Justification* and the *Leuenberg Concord* for the inner-Reformation area.

determines the perspective for the ecumenical work to be dealt with in Catholic/Lutheran efforts and in inner-Reformation efforts on both sides, which form *one* church in the richness of plurality.

Evgeny Pilipenko, whose origins are Russian Orthodox, dealt with a change in perspective that makes possible ecumenical progress. In Orthodoxy the success or failure of ecumenical efforts is closely connected with the importance that is accorded to dogma. The Orthodox Church stresses that unity in dogmatic doctrine is necessary for the unity of the church. Orthodox doctrine, however, secures potentials— such as the recollection of the intention of a process of creating dogma, the dialogical deep rooting of a dogma by its need for reception, and the basic apophatic characteristic of theology—to prove that unity of dogmatic doctrine is not considered in a static manner.

From the stances of the speakers, the discussion concentrated on questions such as, What status does theological teaching have? What is the meaning of consensus? What are legitimate differences? What conditions do the churches set for unity? What limits does a unity of churches have? The Council took as its starting point a basic-existing unity. Still this must be defined in concrete ideas of the goal of ecumenical efforts, especially since in the Council's documents no clear model of unity is to be found. Ecumenical work stands under the precept that not unity is to be established, but the preservation of the division. The already-existing unity from which the Council took its starting point must take form. In this context the detailed comments of Miriam Wijlens offer important help for the interpretation and use of effective canon law.

Recently originating forms of Christianity (autochthonal churches, Pentecostal movements, etc.) demand deepened reflection on ecumenical processes. Within the confessions, fault lines today often run along ethical lines, which are culturally conditioned. The meaning of this for ecumenical relations is to be explained if parts of different confessions agree on such questions and differ from other groups in their respective confessions, groups that, for their part, agree with another group beyond their church boundaries.

Often ecumenical togetherness has become normal for believers. At the same time an indifference is to be observed. Division is seen as given because confessional differences play no important role. Courtesy is often achieved beyond voluntariness because traditional confessional environments break up or newly form.

Finally, the church must—corresponding to the "principle of plurality" (Christoph Theobald)—ask, What is the meaning of the minor significance of confessional differences that are often encountered, especially the "postecumenical" attitude of the younger generation, for the church and ecumenism?

6. *The Church and Judaism*

MEMBERS OF THE PREPARATION TEAM

Prof. Dr. Erwin Dirscherl, Regensburg
Prof. Dr. Maria Neubrand, Paderborn
Prof. Dr. Reinhold Boschki, Tübingen
Professor Dr. DDr. H.c. Josef Wohlmuth, Bonn
PD Dr. René Dausner, Eichstätt

INTERNATIONAL CONSULTANTS

Prof. Dr. Josef Wohlmuth
    Nostra aetate—Legacy and Challenge
Prof. Dr. Reinhold Boschki
    No Memory—No Dialogue: Nostra aetate in the Darkness of Shoa
Prof. Dr. Erwin Dirscherl
    Implications of Nostra aetate 4 regarding the Economy of Salvation
Prof. Dr. Micha Brumlik, Frankfurt/Main
    Attempt to Assess "Nostra Aetate 4" and Its Results with the View of Franz Rosenzweig

COMMENTARY: *Josef Wohlmuth, René Dausner*

1. *Nostra aetate* [NA] 4 is valid as a direction-setting decision, which set in motion a new relation between the church and Judaism. Biblical scholarship read the texts of the Old Testament more deliberately as Jewish texts and recognized in the New Testament writings Jewish handwriting. Jesus himself was a Jew, and the authors of the New Testament, who wrote in Greek, thought in Jewish contexts, which were certainly stamped by the total Middle East including Egypt (and later Athens and Rome). Hebrew bore into the Greek language as a thorn in the flesh (E. Levinas). Texts from Qumran show how ideas of the non-Jewish world were spread in Hebraic and Aramaic Judaism.

   With the revisions of biblical translations, the congress expected a new sensibility to the Jewish tradition in the form of the pre-Christian Bible and contemporary texts of different character. The separation of the Jesus communities was protracted for a long time, and the mutual influence continued.

2. In view of the question of how the relation of Judaism and Christianity should be shaped in the future, Paul plays a decisive role. *Nostra aetate* 4 refers to the influential knowledge of Paul from Romans 9–11. The Vatican "Commission for Religious Relations to Judaism" in its publication of 10 December 2015 selected Romans 11:29 as the heading: "For the gifts and the calling of God are irrevocable." Here the focus is on the faithfulness of God. In addition, two key passages are Romans 9:4–5 (quoted in NA 4) and Romans 11:25–26 central in contemporary Jewish–Christian dialogue. The contemporary exegesis of Paul is characterized by a *New Perspective on Paul:* Paul continued to be a Jew and to remain one.

3. It was thankfully established in the discussion that the impulses of the pope of the Council, John XXIII, were intensified by Pope John Paul II. Theology has taken up these impulses in almost all disciplines and also reflected on them self-critically. The urgent task is to establish the direction-setting decision of the Second Vatican Council in theology and the history of dogma.
4. The final declaration at Munich objects to new forms of (politically oriented) anti-Semitism and anti-Judaism (lurking within the church). Islamic phobia often is connected to anti-Semitism and anti-Judaism. At the same time, according to *Nostra aetate* 4 it is valid that in Jewish–Christian–Islamic dialogue the relation of the church and Judaism is presupposed as an incomparable, unique item. A Christian theology of Judaism therefore will have to set forth still more clearly why the church itself in the future no longer can or wants to understand itself without considering Judaism. This requires a consequential reconsideration in theology of the usual schema "promise–fulfillment," according to which Judaism belongs to a time of shadow, while the church is already in the time of light, of truth, and so lives in the time of fulfillment. The church must remain conscious that it also still looks for fulfillment (LG 48). With Paul, the church hopes that the fulfillment of the promises will occur through the deliverance "of all Israel" (cf. Romans 11:26).
5. At the Council the problematic of "mission to the Jews" was not addressed. The discussion group "Jews and Christians" with the Central Committee of German Catholics, has clearly spoken against mission to the Jews.[6] This position was confirmed by the above-mentioned Vatican declaration of 10 December 2015 in nos. 40–43.

---

6. See H. Frankemölle, J. Wohlmuth, eds., *Das Heil der Anderen: "Problemfeld Judenmission"* (QD 238; Freiburg i. Br., 2010).

6. The congress recognizes the difficulty of conveying the present achievements of the Jewish–Christian conversation to the grassroots church and Jewish communities. The following documents are important on the Christian side: "Guiding Principles and Remarks for the Execution of the Conciliar Declaration "Nostra Aetate" Article 4 (1974)," and "Remarks for a Correct Presentation of Jews and Judaism in Preaching and Catechesis of the Catholic Church" (1985).
7. On the Jewish side the declaration of Jewish scholars *Dabru emet* (Speak truth) of 11 September 2000 still is one of the most important documents. We also appreciate very much the Orthodox Rabbinic Statement on Christianity *To Do the Will of Our Father in Heaven: Toward a Partnership between Jews and Christians* of 3 December 2015, that has been recognized after the congress in Munich.
8. The next topic of dialogue will be more fundamental subjects. (For this a longer list of themes was brought together).
9. The Jewish–Christian dialogue can never pursue the goal of overcoming the original schism (Cardinal Kasper) so that Judaism and Christianity dissolve into one another and surrender their ever-proper call from God. In this regard, Israel J. Yuval (*Zwei Völker in deinem Leib* [Göttingen: Vandenhoeck & Ruprecht, 2007]) has offered a relevant metaphor, describing the relation of Jews and Christians from a new perspective of "recognition." The Italian philosopher Francesco Paolo Ciglia has pointed out the origin of this metaphor in the language of the theater: in the course of a theatrical piece definite roles are revealed step by step; for example, the enemy can be "recognized" as brother. The dramatization of the two people in one body could bring about the knowledge that, after long periods of misunderstanding and hostility, a time of brotherly shalom can come into view for the coming aeon.

7. The Claim of Revelation and the Plurality of Religions

MEMBERS OF THE PREPARATION TEAM

Prof. Dr. Klaus Müller, Münster
Prof. Dr. Magnus Striet, Freiburg i. Br.

INTERNATIONAL CONSULTANTS

AR Dr. Marcello Neri, Flensburg
Reception of Dei Verbum and Nostra Aetate in the USA
Prof. Dr. Giorgio Sgubbi, Lugano
Self-Mediation of God, Necessity, and Freedom. Fundamental Theological Considerations Originating from Dei Verbum
Prof. Dr. Christoph Theobald, Paris
The Claim of Revelation and Pluralism of Religions. On the Reception and Updating of Dei Verbun and Nostra Aetate

COMMENTARY: *Klaus Müller*

The Dogmatic Constitution *Dei Verbum* and the Declaration *Nostra aetate* were the point of departure of the four lectures as well as of the subsequent discussion by the thirty-eight participants within the panel. The decisive task first of all was to work out conceptually the characteristic paradigm of revelation of *Dei Verbum* as God's self-mediation. This concept (it appeared in the 1790s in Carl Immanuel Diez, a student in the Tübingen Stift) was suitable as a topos for the question of the relation of theology and church in the modern age.

The first great attempt at an explanation of this thematic was in the thought of the *Cambridge Platonists* (namely, in the work of Ralph Cudworths). The idea of the Cambridge Platonists is a resource to free the concept of revelation from fideistic and positivistic tendencies.[7]

As concrete goals of the research to be undertaken in exegesis, dogmatics, fundamental theology, and philosophy, the following question-complexes were identified:

1. If revelation is the self-mediation of God's self to the other, it must be totally justified with revelation, which occurs as religion. Exclusiveness, inclusiveness (thus still in the Council's texts), and pluralistic theology of religion altogether undercut the problem that they allege to solve. To continue, it appears to be a reciprocal inclusiveness (in the strict sense): the substantial element of one's own position is expressed more authentically in the symbolic traditions of other religions as in one's own mediality. Basic existing components of foreign religious traditions in their own religious grammar and vocabulary appear more authentic than on their original background. For if one thinks of revelation in the terms suggested by the panel, then the question must be pursued: How do the basic forms of the high religions fit with the structure of human conscience, in whom they shape their respective form?

2. The singularity of Christian revelation must be worked out against this background and will be led, so to speak, through the "eye of the needle" of the incarnation. From Celsus beyond Nietzsche up to Emile Cioran, the sharpest offense is to be taken to the theorem of the incarnation. But to work this out exactly—that God proves his greatest greatness beyond which something greater is not to be thought—places Christian theology in the light of God's self-reduction of the incarnation be-

---

7. See the dispute about Ratzinger's habilitation thesis Part 1.

fore its most challenging task. Some philosophers from Schelling up to Luigi Pareyson and Gianni Vattimo had already anticipated that task before. Johann Georg Hamann and the central didactic play of *Zimzum* offered resources for this task.

3. A central task appears to be how the phrase "And God spoke" is to be discursively opened up. In this respect, a powerful backlog exists theologically, for no "hermeneutical summer" followed the "biblical spring" of the Second Vatican Council.

4. If, according to Rahner, God, through God's self-mediation, becomes the essential part of God's addressees, they are to be determined as co-subjects of the revelatory event. This means that the addressees could only perceive the claim (of revelation) of the Absolute/Infinite within the context of their limited perspective (and with it in a specific refraction).

5. What constitutes the nonderivation of the historical event of revelation in relation to natural relativity in regard to every finite thing at its origin?

6. In view of the joining of God and the human person in the self-mediation, must not necessarily an earlier pantheistic stance as a theorem of the God-question be favored? The difference between God and creation would not be claimed as the final thought, but as a differentiation of the Absolute would be defined. Is the self-mediation as differentiation still in place, God and the human person to be determined in a way suitable to the nature of freedom? More recent linguistic applications, "secular" philosophies (as V. Gerhardt and H. Tetens), raise new challenges for theology.

Only in the medium of the outlined problem-cluster can the connection of the named Council texts to discourse of the modern age be assured.

Through the international cast of consultant sections, (Sgubbi for Italy, Neri for the USA, Theobald for France, and Karimi with the external perspective of Islamic theology), the different reception of the named Council texts became clear.

There is no question for the consultants and women and men in the discussion that the interreligious differences in regard to the concept of revelation must be worked out because, for example, Islam understands revelation primarily as an aesthetic event. The concept of religion as tradition needs a new definition, which concerns the foundations of the philosophy of religion, fundamental theology, and dogmatics. It is valid to work out a supportive theory of religious self-conception. Revelations are then forms of expression of a "theo-andric history" (G. Sgubbi) of God with God's creation.

8. Interreligious Dialogue and Mission

MEMBERS OF THE PREPARATION TEAM

Prof. Dr. Christian Bauer, Innsbruck
Prof. Dr. Margit Eckholt, Osnabrück
Prof. Dr. Michael Sievernich, SJ, Frankfurt
Prof. Dr. Klaus Vellguth, Vallendar/Aachen (Missio)

INTERNATIONAL CONSULTANTS

Prof. Dr. Birgit Weiler, Medical-missionary Sister, Lima/Peru
   Sign of the Time Today: Indigenous Theologies: Threat to the Amazon Region and "Buen vivir". Challenges in Global Perspective
Prof. Dr. Felix Wilfred, Madras/India
   The Reception of Vatican II in Asia
Prof. Dr. Christian Baur, Innsbruck
   The Mission to Serve? Theological Inspirations from Gaudium et spes and Ad gentes

COMMENTARY: *Margit Eckholt*

With the Second Vatican Council the church viewed as "world-church" (Karl Rahner) has come about in a new way. The church can only be characterized in the plurality of cultures, heterogeneity, and fragmentariness of its context. It asks with the search for itself for the world to be itself (Marie-Dominique Chenu). This process acquires form in pastoral care and liturgy, as in independent theological work such as the liberation theologies. The churches of the South have concentrated the concern of Pope John XXIII, Pope Paul VI, and the group "Church of the Poor" on the ways of the poor Jesus in order to find new forms of evangelization.

Mission and diaconia belong together. Because of the carrying out of the church's nature, mission is the task of the whole people of God. It is conversion, starting from each self-centering and thus—according to the kingdom-of-God message of Jesus—diaconia. Fifty years after the Second Vatican Council with Pope Francis a new *kairos* of a *global church interpretation* of the Council has begun. (*Evangelii Gaudium* and *Laudato si'*). "We look forward to a spring of faith and life in Asia" (Felix Wilfred). Mission and diaconia demand a self-removal of borders: a diaconia self-removal of borders in reference to the respective "others," the "poor and distressed of every kind," and the missionary self-removal of borders in regard to their own ecclesial traditions.

Christian Bauer has read in *Gaudium et spes* the aspect of diaconia as the proper innovative impulse and has connected it with the concept of mission in *Ad gentes*. In line with the "presence" of worker-priests in the 1940s in the poor and workers' quarters of the French metropolitan cities, in Latin America one speaks in the 1970s of the *inserción*—the concept of mission begins to change. The key texts form *Ad gentes* 12.

Mission is always unintentionally "self-extravagance to the world" by the gospel here and therein healing and freeing "presence" (Christian Bauer).

The conciliar survey of mission and diaconia must be for the churches of the West a self-understanding matter of course: Around 1960 the Catholic Church worldwide numbered 577 million baptized members. More than half of the Catholics (women and men) lived in Europe and North America. By 2010 the total number of Catholics had more than doubled, and Europe and North America represent not more than one-third of all believers. Catholicism bears the face of the South; in spite of global relief work the German church suffers from a global-ecclesial blindness.

Felix Wilford (Madras/India) indicated that, from the beginning of evangelization, the Asian church has been a "world church." The Asian churches (India, Iran, Central Asia, China, etc.) have enjoyed a "strong autonomy" and have had "at their disposal a diversity of worship services, ways of life, and theologies." Mission has always meant a threefold dialogue: with culture, with religions, and with the poor. Mission was always *missio inter gentes*. The Second Vatican Council caused the Asian churches "to establish missionary societies on the local levels."

Birgit Weiler, a medical-missionary sister in the Peruvian-Amazon area, underlined the purging of characteristically colonial hermeneutics, in order to open the wisdom and ecological traditions of indigenous people. Mission means learning from the other, an "exchange of gifts for mutual enrichment," thus the Indian theologian Eleazar López. It is a question of seeing the "millions of neighbors of another faith in a new light, as part of the plan of the one and only God's revelation and salvation" (F. Wilfred, "The Japanese bishops write to the 'Ecclesia in Asia,'" 1998): "While its doctrine draws from the *kenosis* of Jesus Christ, the church should be modest and open its heart for other religions, so that its understanding of the mystery of Christ is strengthened."

Missio inter gentes, as it has been developed in Asia, always expresses itself in diaconia, in the option for the poor, and in dialogue with cultures and religions.

Now the West has major concerns with the refugees from the Near East and from African and Asian countries, and with their diverse traditions, histories, and religions. Mission is service, solidarity; it grows *inter gentes* from meeting with the many and requires a new binding of mysticism and the political, for intercession for human rights and human dignity, for peace and the preservation of creation. "*Evangelii gaudium*" and "*Laudato si'*" express this: healing presence on the side of the poor and injured creation.

The elaboration of this important element of a new theology of mission is a desideratum for the future.

9. Liturgy and Inculturation

MEMBERS OF THE PREPARATION TEAM

Prof. Dr. Albert Gerhards, Bonn
Prof. Dr. Reinhard Hoeps, Münster
Prof. Dr. Benedikt Kranemann, Erfurt
Prof. Dr. Joachim Schmiedl, Vallendar

INTERNATIONAL CONSULTANTS

Prof. em. Dr. Dr. h.c. Arnold Angenendt, Münster
   The High Prayer and the Post-Consecratory Sacrifice
Prof. Dr. Gerard Rouwhorst, Tilburg
   Inculturation of Liturgy since Vatican II

COMMENTARY: *Benedikt Kranemann, Reinhard Hoeps*

Inculturation

The congress recognizes the unity of the Catholic Church as well as the diversity of rites as an opportunity for a dynamic faith.

In the discussion of the panel there was a broad consensus that the concept of inculturation appears only somewhat suitable to describe the context between liturgy and culture in whose space it is realized. The accompanying schema, at least latent in the concept of inculturation, according to which the liturgy as (fixed) content (in the singular) is introduced in culturally characterized (variable) forms (in the plural), is especially misleading. Nevertheless, culture as well as liturgy provides both content and also formal dimensions: liturgy and culture meet each other in both dimensions.

With the criticism it evokes, the concept of inculturation with regard to liturgy is able to problematize the schema of form and content. Angenendt's statements on post-consecration sacrifice have not finally shown how the figurative concept and the theological argumentation help one another. Therefore, in the analysis of the liturgical event it is barely possible in a meaningful way to distinguish between form and content. To think of liturgy as the genuine interplay of form and content that only artificially permits a division of the one from the other is the constant challenge for theology, whose academic ideal lies elsewhere in the reduction of form to the expression of an abstract content. On the other hand, the liturgy proves itself in this respect a methodological paradigm for theological thought. The range of this paradigm, however, has not been studied in depth.

Culture

The Council has caused an extensive reform of the liturgy in this way. The congress appreciates the profit of this reform for the life of faith and the participation of the faithful.

In the discussion of the panel it was not disputed that the concept of culture in reference to liturgical theology cannot be properly understood in the sense of advanced culture but must involve cultural participation of all layers and groups of a society. This is revealed in all clarity in the liturgical dimensions of language and ritual. With this understanding, the relation of the liturgy to a culture thus understood still is not clearly determined: Should the liturgy itself be expressed in the categories of such a culture (Rouwhorst), or should it be established over against culture as a kind of counterculture (Messner)? A productive debate between these liturgical-theological options does not finally demand a critical assessment of the particular culture in its entirety. In the nontheological area—especially in the present—considerations, impulses, and critical interventions are to be discovered for such an assessment especially in the area of the so-called advanced culture. Therefore, the liturgical-scholarly debate with a preference for an extensive concept of culture is referred for its inspiration and investigation of hypotheses to artistic and theoretical projects of (contemporary) advanced culture.

Further Development of Liturgical Reform

Lively liturgy demands a constant reflection by an inculturated theology, which must be developed in dialogue with culture and study of culture and society.

Because the conception of liturgy is based on the attempt at an authentic and convincing mediation between formal and content elements, the further development of this liturgy is not permitted to be derived from theoretical considerations but demands experiments, in which the evidence from form and shape can be shown and can be examined. The affirmative statement of such experiments is dependent on the concision of its underlying issues and of the quality of the arrangement of its experimental setup. In this regard, proposals and helpful attitudes provide not only related studies of culture and society, but they can also be expected from artistic positions, whose genuine effort is directed to the evident form and authentic expression for (meaningful) perception. Art would then be, for theology, not only a sign of its time and, for the liturgy, not only potential provision of liturgical spaces, but especially a proposal, a critical adversary, and thus a source in the theological discussion of the study of liturgy.

Euro-Centrism

We guarantee that the extensive liturgies of the history of faith as well as of local churches of all continents are to be explored.

The discussion with representatives of African theology in the panel has shown what intense injuries the schema of inculturation has produced in non-European churches. The opposition to foreign influence with European ideas and patterns of thought is still a volatile theme. Christian identity by necessity develops in the context of the respective culture. European Christianity cannot be the standard for the formation of Christian identities on other continents. On the other hand, this insight presents to European theology the central task of reconstructing and reflecting critically on the history and conditions of European culture in its importance for the formation of the proper Christian identity in Europe.

10. Faith and Formation/Education

MEMBERS OF THE PREPARATION TEAM

Prof. Dr. Harald Schwillus, Halle
Prof. Dr. Judith Könemann, Münster

INTERNATIONAL CONSULTANTS

Prof. em. Dr. Dr. h.c. mult. Dietrich Benner, Berlin
Formation/Education "According" to the Second Vatican Council: Concerning Its Relations in view of Pedagogical and Theological Limits of Personal Autonomy, Emancipatory Enlightenment, and Positivist Maturity
Prof. Dr. Monika Jakobs, Lucerne
Faith and Formation/Education according to the Second Vatican Council
Prof. Dr. Cyprian Rogowski, Olsztyn
Faith and Formation/Education in the Secular World: Reflections from a Polish Point of View

COMMENTARY: *Harald Schwillus*

By means of three lectures, the panel at the outset took as a theme the relational network of faith and formation/education.

Dietrich Benner, a scholar of education, first stated that religious truths for their own sake cannot be affirmed only in reference to an authority but also need a plausibility built on principles. Formation/education is necessary to ward off the danger of fundamentalism. Religion is dependent on formation/education, as also formation/education is dependent on religion if it wishes to be complete. Among the conciliar documents, *Gaudium et spes* especially makes possible an opening to this mutual relation.

Benner asks about the pedagogical and theological limits of autonomy, maturity, and elucidation in the area of tension of religious and autonomous morals. The contribution of religious formation/education, as a result of this tension, is to be sought in a way of life that aligns itself in thankfulness to God. It makes possible a discursive self and separate examination, which, with the understanding that the idea of freedom like it is described in *Gaudium et spes* is to be taken seriously. Religion represents an important horizon for human self-understanding. This means that the processes of religious formation/education must hand on basic religious knowledge with attention to the autonomy of the learning—also religious—subject. They are to interpret critically and with the support of reason. Thus, those learning obtain competence for discourse in and about religion. There is here a refusal of an exclusive understanding of the church.

Monika Jakobs, Switzerland, noted the general importance of *aggiornamento* of the Second Vatican Council, which has had a more enduring influenceon the reception of the Council in the area of formation/education than individual Council texts, for example, *Gravissimum educationis*. Since the Council, religious formation and education have become a general educational discourse capable of being related. The Council takes its departure from the idea of a special Catholic society and opens possibilities for a communication of faith with other religions and global views on equal terms. Religious formation/education is perceived by theology and the church as a service that is to be fulfilled for a plural society and that considers the claims of autonomy of the subject. The synod at Würzburg defines religious instruction as a service of the church in the public school that rejects public or concealed intentions of recruitment and wishes to help religion "in matters" in a self-defined formation/education.

In view of a further differentiated religiosity of church members and a declining importance of traditional religion in all of society, new questions are posed. How do theology and church relate to models of religious instruction and formation/education that want to reject an explicitly confessional reference? The so-called social developments in Switzerland lead to the question: Are there forms of formation for internal church catechesis that accept the advancing religious heterogeneity and see it not as a threat but as an opportunity for formation?

The reception of the conciliar documents *Gaudium et spes, Lumen gentium,* and *Gravissimum educationis* in Poland after 1989—thus Cyprian Rogowski—mark an epochal, decisive event that has led to an estrangement of youth and church. For twenty-five years instruction in religion has been introduced in the public schools. This resulted in a clear decline of attendance at parish catechesis. New problems are opened here for the coordination and shaping of religious formation/education in both areas.

The discussion reveals that religious instruction as a central field for religious formation/education forms an important point of contact between church and society. The openness of the church to the world initiated by the Second Vatican Council becomes concrete here. How is religious formation/education legitimated in the contemporary openness of society? At the same time, the clarification of the concept of religion, and of the changes that "religion" experiences in the context of public formation/education, is decisive.

Gaudium et spes and *Lumen gentium* present two perspectives for new connections of education/formation and religion. The Council communicates a productive impulse for the context of faith, religion, and formation/education. In view of a secular world stamped by postmodernity, this *aggiornamento* is to be achieved in relations other than those in the 1960s.

The focal points of the work of reception of the Second Vatican Council, which is to be continued, in the area of formation/education today are the following:

- Theology as a discipline with a faith-connection is to be introduced more clearly in a common process of religious formation/education with its own perspectives, since these cannot be replaced by other perspectives.
- Theology is to be translated into the language(s) of the time.
- It is valid concerning religious instruction to make accessible fields for religious formation/education in postmodern society outside ecclesial interior space.
- The mutual dependence of religion and formation/education is to be made clear.
- The mediation of the "ethic of faith" and "autonomous morals" is to be developed internally from the Christian context: Christian formation/education is the standard of life that enables God's offer to human persons to be able to be accepted in freedom.
- A discursive self-examination and examination of the other belong here.
- The critical potential of religious formation/education—also inside religion—can be raised only if the increase vis-à-vis a mere affirmation of faith is made reasonably accessible.
- Critical religious formation/education establishes in human rights and rights of freedom that which the Second Vatican Council recognizes. In its reception there is the question of a balancing of the autonomy of the (finite) human person and the truths of revelation handed down by tradition.

- In addition there is a need for clear religious competence, which makes possible for the human person the experience and acceptance of the religious dimension of her/his being.
- On the basis of the stance of the Second Vatican Council toward other religions, such processes of religious formation/education are to be expected in all religious communities and, if necessary, are to be supported.

11. *The Church and the Media*

MEMBERS OF THE PREPARATION TEAM

Prof. Dr. Bernd Trocholepczy, Frankfurt/Main
Prof. Dr. Matthias Sellmann, Bochum
Prof. Dr. Hildegard Wustmans, Linz

CONSULTANTS

AR Dr. Jürgen Pelzer, Frankfurt/Main
    Facebook as an Instrument of Aggiornamento: A Theology of Resonance-Experience in Social Media
Prof. Dr. Hildegard Wustmanns, Linz
    Social Media and Recalling of the Council
AR Dr. Jan Kuhn, Bochum
    Authentic Digital Communication: How to Communicate Successfully with Young People about Faith and Religion

COMMENTARY: *Matthias Sellmann, Bernd Trocholepczy*

"Theology sees itself challenged in a special way to make clear the signs of the time"—thus the final declaration of this congress. One wonders which signs of the time today push themselves into the collective consciousness. One will have to name entire areas of themes and challenges of upheavals produced by social information.

First in the 1960s color television arrived; in the 1980s the personal computer; in 1992 the Web 1.0; in 2004 the Web 2.0; in 2007 the smartphone and social networking; and since 2010 the Tablet-PC.

Of higher relevance theologically is that basic ways of reception and production were altered, not simply technically recast. Many authors at the same time referred to a structural similarity of semantics of media and theology. For both originally relate their content and excess of meaning by the observation that something is present in its absence and absent in its presence.

The typical fragmented and extremely complex experience of reality for the postmodern age is enabled, accelerated, and represented by the media. It has become complicated, to reveal virtual reality as nonreality, or to reclaim the methods of authentic interactivity only for physical encounters in the space–time continuum. In order to express it with *Gaudium et spes* and the systematic theologian from Cologne, Hans-Joachim Höhn one can say: It is a sign of the time that we live in a time of signs. These temporal signs are always dominantly produced in the media.

Already a theology that is meaningful for the present must, as the Council demanded it and drafted it (and not only in GS!), bring into the discussion this semantic excess and enormity. This interest is not to be founded simply on the empirical and quantitative dimension of this phenomenon. The understanding of revelation in the Council is shifted from a paradigm of instruction to a paradigm of communication. Revelation is the totally free self-mediation of God to humanity, which seeks beyond the entire system not only the hearer but the interpreter, the person who understands. In this system, communication itself communicates. Revelation is the entrance into the friendly conversation of God with humanity and vice versa (DV 2).

This communicative activity in the understanding of revelation has been counter-read by theology previously in the direction of a technically based media. Point 7 of the declaration of the congress would need to be completed of the understanding of revelation.

This desideratum is now unfortunately reproduced by the thematic point 11 of the declaration but not directly treated in a way that points ahead.

The theological thought is quickly interpreted otherwise in a strategic achievement. The political goal appears to be the more adaptable acting of ecclesial actor in the society of media. In addition, the better the journalistically gifted and up-to-date, the more media-connected is the mediation of faith. Thus, the theology in this passage 11 remains clearly under its post-Vatican intellectual approach.

First and foremost, it was not even recognized that with digital 2.0 communication, the content of that which was communicated with its performance and channels changed. There is not to be communicated first faith and then what is more or less refined. That is the greatest misunderstanding of all those who in the media suppose only a gigantic container. Faith cannot be proclaimed to be proved effective without itself communicating: this means that it first itself produces results—reveals!—when it risks to be self-communicative. If one wants to put it thus: faith is un-nominalized in a social-informative way. Christoph Theobald, in his interpretation of the Council, has designated this as *modus procedendi*, and this he read in the spectacular article 44 from *Gaudium et spes*. This *praedicatio accomodata*—in agreement with the respective linguistic culture that learns, that is, surprises, distresses, and troubles language—is the law of evangelization.

In no. 11 of the declaration it is then further reported: "We are committed to theologically better penetrating the dynamics of media reality, to making it pastorally fruitful, to intensifying dialogue with the secular public, and to activating the inner-ecclesial and theological opinion-forming process and position training more than before."

In addition, one recognizes here that learning is not carried out internally in systematic theology. Instead there is the old model of labor division as though it functioned pastorally thus in a Platonic manner!

The passage commented on here and criticized can become a "beginning of the beginning." The Second Vatican Council possibly becomes also the Vatican 2.0 if the concept of revelation is read radically as a communicative concept and thus again radically as a concept of relation and process. Then theology is un-nominalized; then it will become in its offensive self-variability again credible. But especially then it becomes relevant and affirmatively strong for the creative and politically capable self-interpretation of the human person in a more and more technically determined reality.

12. Creation and Ecology

MEMBERS OF THE PREPARATION TEAM

Prof. Dr. Andreas Lienkamp, Osnabrück
Prof. Dr. Georg Steins, Osnabrück

CONSULTANTS

Prof. Dr. Gerd Weckwerth, Cologne
  Of the "Hymn to Matter," on "The Love of Earth and Its Tangible Becoming": The Environmental Ethics of Teilhard de Chardin: Joining Faith in Creation and Evolution
Prof. Dr. Georg Steins
  "Let her cause righteousness to spring up" (Isa 45:8): Suggestions to Read Biblical Texts on Creation
Prof. Dr. Andreas Lienkamp
  Creation and Ecology in Gaudium et spes: Reading It Anew in a Christian Environmental Perspective

COMMENTARY: *Andraes Lienkamp/Georg Steins*

Corresponding to the anthropological centralism and neglect of nature of their own tradition as well as the technological affinity of the time, the bishops at the Council welcomed the expansion of human hegemony over the environment. The conviction increases that "humanity...can and must ever strengthen its dominion over creation" (GS 9). On the other hand, the pastoral constitution confirms that humanity is *part of* nature (GS 14) and as the image of God (GS 12 and often) has to be involved in wisdom, justice, and love (GS 15, 21 and often) responsibly with creation. Humanity should love the things created by God (GS 37). God's commission is not to transform the earth into a desert but to make it "a dwelling worthy of the whole human family" (GS 57). Thus, the Council takes up a first corrective in the so-called commission of dominion, which was clearly worked out in biblical studies from the 1970s. The commission of creation from Genesis 1 is a commission of protection and custody, which entrusts to all human beings the care for the earth as a home of life.

The *one* ecological-social crisis that begins to take on catastrophic dimensions in the present (see Pope Francis's encyclical *Laudato si'* [2015]) was not grasped in its significance by the bishops of that Council and their theological advisors. Following the Council, the crisis has intensified exponentially. The optimism of progress, which still characterized the Council era, has become questionable with the appearance of the report of the *Club of Rome* about the *Limits of Growth* (1972). Since then the consciousness of the increasing threat to the global ecosystem has grown. *Homo sapiens* are changing the face of the planet; humanity has become a force of destiny for the earth. Paul Crutzen and Eugene F. Stoermer therefore speak of the "anthro-pozan." Thus they express the threat by human beings to the earthly space of life but also their special responsibility for all.

Time presses! The climate change caused by human beings, the destruction of forests, the devastation of wetlands and coral reefs, the reduction of the quality of soil, the contamination of water and air with poisonous substances, the accumulation of harmful materials in animals, the wholesale death of species, the expansion of deserts, and the stagnation and overfishing of the oceans are central symptoms of the environmental crisis. At the same time, the poor and future generations are most intimately affected.

Theologians are required to support actively the urgent, necessary processes of transformation in the direction of sustainability. It is valid for global society to regain lost balances: between human beings and their fellow creatures, between market and state, between economy and politics, between acceleration and slowness, between individual and society, and between men and women, as well as between short and long term, local and global, and particular and holistic thought. A rich potential for this change is found in the traditions of wisdom of the Bible, in the history of the church as well as in the indigenous theologies and practices of the good—that is, the sufficient—life (*buen vivir/sumaq kawsay*).

The classical strengths of theology in protology, soteriology, and eschatology, anthropology and ethics, ecclesiology, and pastoral theology stand thus before a new "sign of the time." It is a question of the survival of our civilization and countless fellow-creatures as well as the habitable condition of the earth. "In view of the urgency of the problem, the Catholic Church has lagged behind what is possible and necessary. With regard to [theological] reflection and [ecclesial] practice...a considerable backlog exists" (DBK: Der Klimawandel: Brennpunkt globaler, intergenerationeller und ökologischer Gerechtigkeit, 2007, Nr. 59 [Climate Change: Focal Point of Global, Intergenerational and Ecological Justice]). Therefore the signatories of the final declaration of the Munich congress committed themselves to the preservation of creation and to place at the center of theological work ecological questions. This is for the theological prime movers neither optional nor secondary but obligatory. For theology, with the choice of its topics, there are questions of priority: Is it concerned with incidental and fashionable questions or with questions that are relevant and important for survival?

If theology is properly to handle its "topics" creation and ecology, it must exchange views with the natural sciences. At the same time, it has the task to stand up to a secular naturalism and also to a fundamentalistic creationism (including the pseudo-science variety of "intelligent design"). *Gaudium et spes* has already made reference to Teilhard de Chardin. The quasi-official ecclesial recognition of the theory of evolution occurred first through Pope John Paul II (message of 29 November 1996 to the Papal Academy of Sciences). The coordination of natural sciences and faith still represents one of the central tasks of present and future theology. The dialogue appears presently very fragile. Not least of all, the classical and newer stances of process theology could enrich the determination of the relation of God, humanity, and nature. Theology must rethink the basic concept of its doctrine of creation and translate it into a secular context in order to remain capable of communication.

The tasks and contexts of crisis change the view of the Council and at the same time sharpen the perception and appreciation of its accomplishments and limits. Among the conciliar documents that are to be underscored for a rereading is *Gaudium et spes,* the chief reference. This text, as no other conciliar text, turns to the topics of creation and ecology. Also important, however, are the second constitution on the church, *Lumen gentium*, according to which the *ecclesia universalis* is a sacrament of salvation and as such should be active in the world, and the constitution on revelation *Dei Verbum*, which gives notice to the recently discovered fullness of the biblical witness. In view of the responsibility of the total human family, one can expect important stimulations from the decrees, such as the declarations on the laity, on ecumenism, and on non-Christian religions.

The following questions and tasks of research must be addressed in the future more extensively than they have been until now. How can the *one* ecological-social crisis be understood more strongly as a sign of the time and be included in theological reflection? What is the importance of the new definition of the role of humanity in society and nature for the hermeneutic of the Council? Is the Vatican Council really as anthropo-centered, neglectful of nature, and optimistic of progress as it appears at first glance? What contribution does the theological category "creation" make in the present scholarly discourse? What plausibility does it have and what potentials could be coordinated with it in the current debate? What is the importance of the category of the sacrament of salvation of the church? On the horizon of ecological threat and responsibility for creation, how are the pedagogy of pastoral care and religion changed? Who are the subjects of a new spirituality of creation and of a strengthened engagement with the environment? How are soteriology, eschatology, and apocalypticism to be understood in the light of this background? How does the biblical heritage of the narratives of creation and wisdom theology make new alignments of theological ethics as individual-social-environmental ethics as well as for interreligious and intercultural understanding?

CONCLUSION

Over a period of several years, more than forty theologians were actively engaged in preparing this International Congress. Without the commitment of so many colleagues it would not have been possible to work out in advance all these different issues that were intensively discussed during the congress. In the name of the congress team we would therefore like to offer our sincere thanks.

We would particularly like to thank all the speakers who contributed to the congress's success with their lectures and their leading of different workshops that sharpened the preceding presentations. Meanwhile, all articles have been published in a comprehensive collection: *Vaticanum 21: Die bleibende Aufgabe des Zweiten Vatikanischen Konzils im 21. Jahrhundert. Dokumentationsband zum Münchner Kongress "Das Konzil 'eröffnen,'"* edited by Christoph Böttigheimer and René Dausner, with Franz Xaver Bischof, Marianne Heimbach-Steins, Peter Hünermann, Benedikt Kranemann, Johanna Rahner, Joachim Schmiedl, and Josef Wohlmuth (Freiburg i. Br.: Crossroad / Herder & Herder, 2016). This International Congress has been successful in pointing out the relevance of the Second Vatican Council in the present time involving all theological disciplines. Commenting on the formal end of the Second Vatican Council, Karl Rahner said at that time: "Indeed it will take a long time until the Church which has been given the Second Vatican Council by God will be the Church of the Second Vatican Council.". Rahner, who spoke about "the beginning of a beginning" in this context, should be proved right: reception and implementation of the Second Vatican Council can by no means be considered to have been completed.

As a result of the congress, the final statement, signed by a significant number of theologians, has received a great deal of approval. We hope that the intention of the Second Vatican Council will have an impact on both the prospective theological research and the church in order to be prepared for all relevant issues concerning the twenty-first century and to find adequate answers to these issues in the Council's spirit.

The Editors

LIST OF PRIMARY SIGNATORIES

(As of 22 April 2016)

Arnold, Claus, Prof. Dr., Frankfurt
Arntz, Norbert, Cleves
Autiero, Antonio, Prof. Dr., Münster
Bauer, Christian, Prof. Dr., Innsbruck
Benz, Brigitte, Erfurt
Boschki, Reinhold, Prof. Dr., Tübingen
Bosschaert, Dries, Leuven
Brosseder, Hubert, Prof. Dr., Unterhaching
Büchner, Christine, Prof. Dr., Hamburg
Demel, Sabine, Prof. Dr., Regensburg
Derksen, Nicolas J. M., Dr.
Doss, Jude Nirmal
Eckholt, Margit, Prof. Dr., Osnabrück
Engel, Ulrich, Prof. Dr., Berlin
Essen, Georg, Prof. Dr., Bochum
Faber, Eva-Maria, Prof. Dr., Chur
Faggioli, Massimo, Prof. Dr., St. Paul, Minnesota/USA
Fischer, Luisa, Mainz
Häfner, Gerd, Prof. Dr., Munich
Hagedorn, Jonas, Darmstadt
Hark, Norbert, Dr., Katzenfurt
Haunerland, Winfried, Prof. Dr., Munich
Hegewald, Birigt, Dr., Osnabrück
Heyder, Regina, Dr., Mainz
Hinze, Bradford E., Prof. Dr., New York
Hoeps, Reinhard, Prof. Dr., Münster
Holzbrecher, Sebastian, Dr., Erfurt
Jakobs, Monika, Prof. Dr., Lucerne
Keiling, Siegbert, Munich
Kirsten, Elke, Dr., Oberndorf
Kintsurashvili, Shota
Klasen, Brigitte
Knobloch, Stefan, Prof. Dr., Mainz/Passau
Knoll, Alfons, Prof. Dr., Regensburg
Kruip, Gerhard, Prof. Dr., Mainz
Kuhn, Jan, Bochum
Lampe, Armando, Prof. Dr., Frankfurt/Mexico
Lienkamp, Andreas, Prof. Dr., Osnabrück

Link, Hans-Georg, Dr., Cologne
Lintner, Martin, Dr., Innsbruck
Loretan, Adrian, Prof. Dr., Lucerne
Mack, Elke, Prof. Dr., Erfurt
Madragule Badi, Jean-Bertrand, P. Dr. Dr., OP
Mandry, Christof, Prof. Dr., Frankfurt
Maurer, Richard, Munich
Mayer, Annemarie C., Prof. Dr., Leuven
Meier, Johannes, Prof. Dr., Mainz
Mpanga, Denis
Mueller, Klaus, Prof. Dr. Dr., Münster
Mueller-Geib, Werner, Prof. Dr., Bad Kreuznach
Nawar, Alexander, PD Dr., Mainz
Neubrand, Maria, Prof. Dr., Paderborn
Neuner, Peter, Prof. em. Dr., Vaterstetten
Nientiedt, Ruth, Mainz
Olisaemeka, Lotanna, Koblenz/Nigeria
Ramos-González, Cristino, Tübingen/Paraguay
Renz, Andreas, Dr., Munich
Rheinbay, Georg, Dr., Bernau
Rouwhorst, Gerard, Prof. Dr., Tilburg/Niederlande
Ruh, Ulrich, Freiburg
Salaske, Sebastian, Münster
Samson, Judith, Dr., Bochum
Sander, Hans-Joachim, Prof. Dr., Salzburg
Schramm, Michael, Prof. Dr., Hohenheim
Schuppe, Florian, Dr., Munich
Schwillus, Harald, Prof. Dr., Halle
Sellmann, Matthias, Prof. Dr., Bochum
Spalink, Gerwin, Munich
Steins, Georg, Prof. Dr., Münster
Sutor, Bernhard, Prof. Dr., Eichstätt
Theobald, Christoph, Prof. Dr., Paris
Trocholepczy, Bernd, Prof. Dr., Frankfurt
Tschorn, Christopher, Erfurt
Vellguth, Klaus, Prof. Dr. mult., Aachen
Viehoff, Helmut, Hamburg
Voges, Stefan, Dr., Aachen
Völlmy, Annina, Liestal
Vutz, Johannes, Paderborn
Weber, Stephan, Dr., Freiburg
Werbick, Jürgen, Prof. Dr., Münster
Weiler, Birgit, Prof. Dr., Peru
Witting, Caroline, Mainz

LIST OF CO-SIGNATORIES
(As of 22 April 2016)

Arens, Edmund, Prof. Dr., Lucerne/Switzerland
Ansorge, Dirk, Prof. Dr., Sankt Georgen
Bärsch, Jürgen, Prof. Dr., Eichstätt
Baumann, Urs, Prof. em. Dr., Rottenburg/N
Becker, Patrick, Dr., Aachen
Beinert, Wolfgang, Prof. Dr., Pentling
Bernard, Felix, Prof. h.c. Dr., Osnabrück
Bieberstein, Sabine, Prof. Dr., Eichstätt
Biesinger, Albert, Prof. Dr., Bühl
Birkel, Simone, Dr., Eichstätt
Bitter, Gottfried, Prof. Dr., Remagen
Böntert, Stefan, Prof. Dr., Bochum
Brieden, Norbert, Dr., Wuppertal
Bucher, Rainer, Prof. Dr., Graz
Cebulj, Christian, Prof. Dr., Chur
Dell'Oro, Roberto, Prof. Dr., Los Angeles, California
Disse, Jörg, Prof. Dr. Dr., Fulda
Eicher, Peter, Prof. Dr. Dr., Fribourg
Emunds, Bernhard, Prof. Dr., Frankfurt
Engel, Ulrich, Prof. Dr., OP, Berlin
Engshuber, Maria, Hinterschmiding
Franz, Albert, Prof. Dr., Dresden
Freitag, Josef, Prof. Dr., Erfurt
Frevel, Christian, Prof. Dr., Bochum
Garhammer, Erich, Prof. Dr., Würzburg
Gerhards, Albert, Prof. Dr., Bonn
Görtz, Heinz-Jürgen, Prof. Dr., Barsinghausen
Groen, Basilius Jacobus, Prof. Dr., Graz
Gruemme, Bernhard, Prof. Dr., Bochum
Haslinger, Herbert, Prof. Dr., Paderborn
Hauser, Linus, Prof. Dr., Gießen
Heidemann, Astrid, Dr., Wuppertal
Heinz, Gerhard, Seminarprof. i.R., Dr., Speyer

Henze, Barbara, Dr., Freiburg
Hoff, Gregor Maria, Prof. Dr., Salzburg
Hofer, Peter, Regensburg
Irsigler, Hubert, Prof.em. Dr., Ebringen
Jäggle, Martin, Prof. i.R. Dr., Vienna
Kaplánek, Michal, Dr., Cˇeské Budeˇjovice
Karrer, Leo, Prof. em., Fribourg
Kessler, Hans, Prof. em. Dr., Frankfurt
Kießling, Klaus, Prof. Dr. Dr., Frankfurt
Kirchschläger, Walter, Prof. Dr., Lucerne
Kirschner, Martin, Dr., Tübingen
Klöckener, Martin, Prof. Dr., Fribourg
König, Otto, Ao. Prof. i.R., Dr., Graz
Kohle, Hubert, Sulzberg
Kohler Spiegel, Helga, Prof. Dr., A-Feldkirch
Kos, Elmar, Prof. Dr., Vechta
Kroth, Jürgen, Dr., Urbar
Kropacˇ, Ulrich, Prof. Dr., Eichstätt
Lesch, Walter, Prof. Dr., Louvain-la-Neuve
Luthe, Heinz-Otto, Prof. Dr., Eichstätt
Lutterbach, Hubertus, Prof. Dr. Dr., Essen
Lutz-Bachmann, Matthias, Prof. Dr. Dr., Frankfurt
Mendl, Hans, Prof. Dr., Passau
Mette, Norbert, Prof. i.R. Dr. Dr. h.c., Münster

Mueller, Christine, Osnabrück
Mooney, Hilary, Prof. Dr., Weingarten
Mommertz, Paul, Munich
Neufing, Teresa, Halle
Pauly, Wolfgang, Prof. Dr., Hainfeld
Pelzer, Jürgen, Dr. des., Frankfurt
Pemsel-Maier, Sabine, Prof. Dr., Freiburg
Predel, Gregor, Prof. Dr., Fulda
Prueller-Jagenteufel, Gunter, Prof. Dr., Vienna
Radlbeck-Ossmann, Prof. Dr., Halle
Redtenbacher, Andreas, Prof. Dr., Vallendar
Reichardt, Deiter, Hinterschmiding
Rethmann, Albert-Peter, Dr., Koblenz
Reuter, Wolfgang, Prof. Dr., Vallendar
Rogowski, Cyprian, Prof. Dr., Olsztyn/Polen
Rosenberger, Michael, Prof. Dr., Linz
Rothe, Daniel, Mainz
Ruhstorfer, Karlheinz, Prof. Dr., Dresden
Sailer-Pfister, Sonja, JProf. Dr., Vallendar
Schambeck, Mirjam, Prof. Dr., Freiburg
Scherzberg, Lucia, Prof. Dr., Saarbrücken
Schnabl, Christa, Prof. Dr., Vienna
Schockenhoff, Eberhard, Prof. Dr., Freiburg

List of Primary Signatories

Sedlak, Katharina, Düren
Seidl, Alois, Hinterschmiding
Seigfried, Adam, Prof. Dr., Regensburg
Siebenrock, Roman, Prof. Dr., Innsbruck
Sievernich SJ, Michael, Prof. Dr., Frankfurt
Sirovátka, Jakub, Prof. Dr., Prague/Budweis
Specker SJ, Tobias, JProf. Dr., Frankfurt
Stosch, Klaus von, Prof. Dr., Paderborn
Stica, Petr, Dr., Münster
Stinglhammer, Hermann, Prof. Dr., Passau
Stritar, Gottfried, Dekan i.R., Truchtlaching
Strohe, Jürgen, Koblenz
Treitler, Wolfgang, Ao. Univ.-Prof., Dr., Vienna
Uhrig, Christian, Dr., Essen
Vellguth, Klaus, Prof. Dr. mult., Aachen
Walter, Peter, Prof. i.R., Dr., Freiburg
Weß, Paul, Univ. Doz. Dr. Dr., Innsbruck
Wessely, Christian, ao. Prof. Dr., Graz
Weiss, Andreas, Prof. Dr., Eichstätt
Wendel, Saskia, Prof. Dr., Cologne
Wucherpfennig, Ansgar, Prof. Dr., Sankt Georgen
Wustmans, Hildegard, Prof. Dr., Linz
Zieroff, Gabriele, PD Dr., Regensburg

ALPHABETICAL INDEX OF AUTHORS

Franz Xaver Bischof, born 1955, Professor of Church History (Middle Ages and modern times), University of Munich

Christoph Böttigheimer, born 1960, Professor of Fundamental Theology, Catholic University of Eichstätt-Ingolstadt

Thomas Bremer, born 1957, Professor of Ecumenism, Eastern Church Studies and Peace Research, University of Münster

René Dausner, born 1975, Privatdozent of Fundamental Theology, Catholic University of Eichstätt-Ingolstadt

Margit Eckholt, born 1960, Professor of Dogmatics and Fundamental Theology, University of Osnabrück

Gerd Häfner, born 1960, Professor of Introduction to the Old and New Testament, University of Munich

Marianne Heimbach-Steins, born 1959, Professor of Christian Social Science, University of Münster

Reinhard Hoeps, born 1954, Professor of Catholic Theology and Its Didactics, University of Münster

Peter Hünermann, born 1929, Professor em. of Dogmatics, University of Tübingen

Gerhard Kruip, born 1957, Professor of Christian Anthropology and Social Ethics, University of Mainz

Andreas Lienkamp, born 1962, Professor of Christian Social Science, University of Osnabrück

Klaus Müller, born 1955, Professor of Philosophical General Questions of Theology, University of Münster

Johanna Rahner, born 1962, Professor of Dogmatics, History of Dogma, and Ecumenical Theology, University of Tübingen

Harald Schwillus, born 1962, Professor of Religious Education, University of Halle-Wittenberg

Matthias Sellmann, born 1966, Professor of Pastoral Theology, University of Bochum

Georg Steins, born 1959, Professor of Biblical Theology and Exegesis of the Old Testament, University of Osnabrück

Saskia Wendel, born 1964, Professor of Systematic Theology, University of Cologne

Maria Wernsmann, born 1982, assistant lecturer, University of Münster

Josef Wohlmuth, born 1938, Professor em. of Dogmatics, University of Bonn

www.ingramcontent.com/pod-product-compliance
Lightning Source LLC
Chambersburg PA
CBHW021003230426
43666CB00005B/262